THE
CHANGING
MAN

Dr Cate Howell is a GP, therapist, educator and author. She is the recipient of a Churchill Fellowship and completed a PhD on depression. In 2012 Cate was awarded the Order of Australia Medal for services to mental health. Cate has worked extensively as a General Practitioner with Defence, and currently has a private practice focusing on mental health and is involved in various teaching activities. Cate has a passion for sharing practical information about mental health through writing, and she has authored five books on mental health and counselling.

Alex Barnard is an educator and musician, and Cate Howell's son. He has been passionate about mental health and wellbeing since he was a teenager, especially anxiety and depression prevention and intervention. During his final year at the Victorian College of the Arts, where he studied a Bachelor of Music Performance, his major research assessment focused on performance anxiety in musicians and the physical and psychological strategies used to overcome it. Alex's goal is to study Music Therapy and assist individuals to improve their mental health and wellbeing through music.

THE CHANGING MAN

A MENTAL HEALTH MANUAL

DR CATE HOWELL OAM, CSM, CF
& ALEX BARNARD

Empower

practical self-help tools by leading experts

First published 2020
This edition published 2023

Exisle Publishing Pty Ltd
PO Box 864, Chatswood, NSW 2057, Australia
226 High Street, Dunedin, 9016, New Zealand
www.exislepublishing.com

A CiP record for this book is available from the National Library of Australia.

978-1-922539-62-5

Designed by Shaun Jury
Typeset in Miller Text Roman 9.5/14pt
The illustration on page 37 was created by Shaun Jury, inspired by
Shutterstock 302782661
Printed in China

This book uses paper sourced under ISO 14001 guidelines from well-managed forests
and other controlled sources.

10 9 8 7 6 5 4 3 2 1

Disclaimer
This book is a general guide only and should never be a substitute for the skill,
knowledge and experience of a qualified medical professional dealing with the facts,
circumstances and symptoms of a particular case. The nutritional, medical and health
information presented in this book is based on the research, training and professional
experience of the authors, and is true and complete to the best of their knowledge.
However, this book is intended only as an informative guide; it is not intended to
replace or countermand the advice given by the reader's personal physician. Because
each person and situation is unique, the authors and the publisher urge the reader to
check with a qualified healthcare professional before using any procedure where there
is a question as to its appropriateness. The authors, publisher and their distributors
are not responsible for any adverse effects or consequences resulting from the use
of the information in this book. It is the responsibility of the reader to consult a
physician or other qualified healthcare professional regarding their personal care. The
intent of the information provided is to be helpful; however, there is no guarantee of
results associated with the information provided.

This book is dedicated to Fred.

CONTENTS

INTRODUCTION

It always seems impossible until it's done.
Nelson Mandela

Whoever you are and whatever reasons you may have, it's great that you are seeking information or help through this book. In terms of mental health, men are affected by everyday stress, high workloads, anxiety and depression, loss of confidence or identity, relationship breakdown, family disruption, addictions and trauma to name a few. And men have found it hard to seek help in the past because of a sense of shame that, in fact, stems from the society we live in. We know that too many men are suffering in silence, and male suicide rates are very high. If you watch the media, you will regularly hear the current worrying statistics about men and mental health issues.

Written for men of all ages, *The Changing Man* provides a collection of tried and tested tools to tackle mental health issues. The book aims to help men become as resilient as possible in life, to prevent issues from arising in the first instance, or stopping them from recurring. There are not a huge number of resources available for men, and the majority seem to be on building muscles and not much else! This is an indication of the sort of messages society gives about what it is to be a man. However, men deserve more than this and *need* more than this.

Thankfully, times and men are changing! They are redefining what it is to be a man and reaching out for information about themselves and the life issues they are experiencing. Not too long ago, I took an Uber to go to an event. The first driver, who was 37 years of age, told me that he and his wife were thinking about having a family, but he wasn't confident about being a father. We talked through his concerns. The driver on the way home was 23 years of age. He was working two jobs and saving up for some things he wanted in life. He asked, 'Do you have any wisdom to share on life?' I suppose my silver-grey hair has an air of knowing about it, so I shared some thoughts with him about focusing on what is important to him in life and making sure to live in the moment as much as possible!

These young drivers were wanting to talk about life and searching for some answers. If you are reading this book, no doubt this applies to you as well. In the past few years, more and more men have booked in to my practice for some assistance. They have been looking for answers as to why they are struggling with their emotions or problems in life, and they have been open to learning about ways to improve how they are feeling and functioning, and seeking change.

Over my 30 years as a medical practitioner, I have studied, practised and taught in the fields of medicine, mental health and therapy, both in Australia and overseas, and have been recognized with various awards. I have done a great deal of work with people in the armed forces, the majority of whom have been male. I have seen many who have viewed being a man and a serving member as needing to be incredibly strong, and many who have been affected by significant trauma from their time in service. However, emerging from their suffering has been a new definition of 'courage' — being aware of the issues, seeking assistance with their mental health and dealing with the issues and the related emotions.

In addition, I have a vested interest in men's wellbeing. On a personal level, I was very close to my father, and I was very involved in his care in the years before his death. I am also very fortunate to have a son, Alex, who I have learnt a lot from by raising him with his father. And I have a male partner in life.

The Changing Man has been a joint project for Alex and me. Alex is a professional musician and very creative. He is also very interested in men's mental health. This has stemmed from undertaking some studies in psychology and having an empathetic nature. Alex has supported friends with mental health issues, and we have both had to tackle anxiety in one form or another in our personal lives.

Alex has helped to research this book due to this interest, and he has contributed significantly to the writing. In particular, he has brought a young man's perspective to the content, and you will find that he has given his voice to a series of tips, which you will see throughout the chapters.

The aim of a doctor or therapist is to provide a safe place for people to talk, explore and to learn some helpful techniques. Hopefully you will see this book as a safe place too. It is written as though we are simply talking — sometimes questions are posed to you, and possible answers are offered. I say 'possible' because no one has all the answers, and everyone's situation is different. Remember that you are the expert on yourself, and this book aims to add to your existing knowledge.

Although the focus of this book is on mental health and wellbeing, you will find that some information on physical wellbeing is also included. This is because both physical and mental health are important and they impact each other.

Interestingly, people seem to more easily recognize the need to look after their physical fitness, and the value of working on one's mental fitness is not as well recognized. Consider that the contents of this book can give you many good ideas for regular mental health 'workouts', to improve your sense of wellbeing.

Working on and improving your mental health involves practice and change but, as we all know, change is hard. Key points and lists have been included in the book, so it is easier to access the information. We have also adopted the idea of a 'toolkit', with a range of tips and tools listed to help you manage life's ups and downs. This allows you to read the book from start to finish or you can dip into it whenever and wherever you choose. The different types of tools in the book address various issues including stress and anxiety, unhelpful thinking habits or behaviours in life, managing uncomfortable emotions, coping in times of change or challenge, preventing relapses, and improving your general wellbeing.

In terms of the different psychological approaches and tools outlined in this book, remember that 'no one size fits all'. The intention is to lay them out in front of you so that you can explore them all and decide which ones fit best for you. You can then choose which ones to put into your toolkit, so they are ready to pull out and put into action as you need to.

We cannot cover all the issues related to men's mental health in this manual, but we have picked out some of the main ones, and many resources are provided at the end of the book. We have endeavoured to find reputable and useful resources originating from a range of countries to suit readers everywhere. Sometimes this has been challenging for a particular topic, but we hope that you can benefit from the resources we have managed to locate. We have favoured quality over quantity.

We live in a constantly changing world which at times is very stressful. Mental health issues are increasingly common, and they can affect our lives significantly or cause loss of life. There are still many barriers to overcome in relation to society's messages about what it is to be male, and about seeking help when there is distress. Fortunately, we are starting to tackle these barriers and remove them. *The Changing Man* is part of these endeavours, so let's get on with it!

1.

ABOUT MEN'S MENTAL HEALTH

If you can change your mind, you can change your life.
William James

Having some knowledge about men's mental health gives you a greater understanding of some of its challenges and may help to empower you to possibly go a bit easier on yourself and to take some action towards change.

The key to understanding men's mental health is exploring the meaning of 'masculinity' or what it is to be a man. Equally, we need to consider the negative impact of shame in men's lives, because overcoming shame is one of the most important areas in men's mental health.

In this chapter, we will look at the issues affecting men's mental health, and in the chapters that follow we will build on this information with many practical ideas and tools.

WHAT'S THE STORY WITH MENTAL HEALTH?

We often take our health for granted, but it is central to feeling good about ourselves, both physically and mentally. When you have the flu or a painful injury, you realize how important your physical health is. Equally, when you feel emotionally exhausted or down, you realize how important your mental health is to your sense of wellbeing.

According to the World Health Organization (2014): 'mental health is a state of well-being in which an individual realizes his or her own abilities, can cope with the normal stresses of life, can work productively and is able to make a contribution to his or her community.'[1] It involves our emotions (feelings), thoughts and behaviours (actions). *The Oxford Dictionary* defines wellbeing as a state of being 'comfortable, healthy or happy'. So, who doesn't want more wellbeing?

Psychologist Abraham Maslow talked about a 'hierarchy of needs' and said that, for humans to reach their potential, they need to meet various needs. These needs range from basic needs (food, warmth, shelter and security), psychological needs (belonging, love and esteem), to self-fulfillment. We need to have our very basic needs met to be able to achieve the higher needs.

Maslow's Hierarchy of Needs

Maslow's model leads into the idea that a range of factors influence health, and that maintaining your health and wellbeing needs a 'whole person' approach, focusing on all aspects of 'you', including:

- Your physical self.
- Your emotional wellbeing.
- Your social self (relationships and connections with others, living situation and finances).
- Your cultural identity (cultural heritage, dealing with racism).
- Gender-related aspects of you.
- Your occupations (what you do in relation to leisure or work).
- Your spiritual life (religion or spirituality, finding meaning in life).

To illustrate what it means to take a 'whole person' approach, let's look at the story of a man called Alfred, who was going through very significant physical and mental health issues:

An occupational therapist was asked to see a man in his sixties called Alfred. He was from the remote outback of Australia, had recently had a heart attack and was recovering in hospital. He was feeling depressed as a result. He was descended from Afghani camel traders and as a young boy had learnt to create leather whips and saddles for camels — skills he had not used for many years.

At the same time, the therapist was asked to see two young men in the hospital's burns unit, both of whom had burns to their arms. She got the men together and asked Alfred to teach the young men some leather work, as this activity would help function to return to their arms.

Alfred obliged over several weeks and the change in both him and the young men was remarkable. By doing something of value and tapping into his creative skills again, Alfred's depression improved, and he returned home after his rehabilitation. The younger men recovered well too.

You can see that Alfred's past story was very important, and what helped him recover was addressing him as a 'whole person'. He was helped to connect with the young men, and to feel more empowered by teaching them some of his valuable skills. He regained a sense of purpose and identity, and his mental health improved greatly.

MEN HAVE VARIOUS LIFE STAGES

It can be helpful to remember that men age in 'stages'. As a man ages, he heads into the middle years and then moves into the more senior years. These stages involve growing as a person. A young man is physically in his prime, usually becomes independent, finds his path in life, and possibly a partner. As a man moves towards middle age, life often becomes more secure, and he gains both experience and wisdom. An older man in his senior years tends to share his wisdom, pursue his interests and enjoy his family.

At each stage, there can be joy, such as starting a first job or becoming a father. There can also be many challenges, such as relationship issues, or finding a sense of worth after retirement. In the later stages of life, older men face their own mortality and experience various losses (such as health issues or the death of friends or loved ones).

Depending on your age and stage, there might be different

parts of this book that speak to you. So please focus on the different parts of the book that you think are most useful.

WHAT DO WE KNOW ABOUT MEN AND MENTAL HEALTH?

Men and women have the same range of feelings but are taught by society to express and deal with them in different ways (more on this in a moment). Anyone can develop mental health issues, leading to mild or severe distress and possibly a negative effect on how they function in their day-to-day life. Here are some facts and figures about men's mental health:

- Men experience a range of mental health issues, such as depression, insomnia (difficulty sleeping), anxiety, schizophrenia (an illness with psychotic symptoms including hallucinations and disturbances to thinking), substance-related issues, autism, dementia and post-traumatic stress disorder.
- Suicide rates in men are three times higher than for women and are a leading cause of death in young men globally.[2]
- Substance use occurs at a rate of 3 to 1 in comparison to females.
- Young men suffer some of the most serious mental health issues, but many stay silent. Only 13 per cent of young men seek help for mental health issues.[3]
- There are higher rates of some mental health issues in homosexual men, such as mood disorders including depression and bipolar disorder, some forms of anxiety, and eating disorders. Bisexual men are also at greater

risk. Social stigma is thought to have a significant impact on the mental health of individuals identifying as gay, trans-sexual or with another gender or sexual identity.[4]

- A key issue is that men are less likely than women to seek help for mental health issues, and they may delay or avoid getting help. Gay men, however, are more likely to seek assistance.

KEY POINT

Men are less likely than women to seek help for mental health issues due to many social stigmas that surround men's mental health, such as feeling shame or the expectation that they be in control and not appear to be 'weak'. We need to change this.

There are a number of potential barriers that stop men from seeking help:

- Ideas about masculinity and that being male means being 'strong' and having emotional issues or seeking help might mean being 'weak'.
- The presence of mental health issues may mean 'not being competent enough' to solve the problem, 'not in control', or being vulnerable, and this might trigger a sense of shame.
- The stigma that exists in the community about mental health issues in general.

- Men seem to have greater difficulty in recognizing emotions than women, in part because of how they have been taught to push feelings down when growing up, and because they may experience emotions in different ways. Men are more likely to notice the physical symptoms of emotional distress before the emotional ones, so they may not realize they have mental health issues.

- When a man recognizes that there is a problem, he may decide to get help, but when he reaches out, he may feel very uncomfortable talking about his mental health. He may say 'no' to the help that is offered because of the reasons mentioned above.

Here is a story about a young man who found it difficult to recognize and express how he was feeling:

A 30-year-old soldier called Nate was directed to see a doctor on his military base by his senior officer, who had noticed Nate was withdrawn and angrier than usual. Nate denied any issues and answered 'no' to almost all the questions asked, so it was difficult for the doctor to assess what was going on.

The doctor organized to see him again two days later, by which time Nate was feeling very distressed and tearful. He was able to acknowledge that he was 'not okay' and had been feeling angry, very tired, was not sleeping well, and was struggling to relate to his partner. His greatest fear was being perceived as 'weak' by his colleagues. Nate and the doctor were able to identify that depression was the underlying problem.

There are also differences between men and women in terms of their nervous system. When women experience an emotion, the part of the brain responsible for the emotion (the limbic system) communicates with the parts of the brain responsible for language. Therefore, they are more able to talk about how they feel. In men, the emotional part of the brain communicates with the body, so men tend to feel the emotion in their body and express it through behaviours. A young man may feel angry and he expresses the feeling by hitting a wall, for example, rather than expressing the feeling in words.[5]

MASCULINITY

If you ask a young man about the male qualities they desire, they will often say to be strong, athletic, muscular, tall, have a job/career, be sporty, be sexually attractive, and so on. Where does this come from? A lot has to do with all the influences on boys and young men growing up (such as their families, school, religion and media to name a few), and the gender expectations in society.

Professor and author Brené Brown identifies a number of key ideas about masculinity in her research, including work being central to identity and being in control of emotions. Young boys are often taught not to express how they feel, but to fix the problem: 'Don't cry if you can't hit the ball, just hit it (and) harder.' And various cultures have different expectations and norms on how boys should behave.[6]

There have also been traditional ideas about what it is to be a man, such as being courageous, being in control, being the 'breadwinner' in a family or a protective father. Some of these ideas have had positive effects, but some have had negative effects, such as pushing emotions down or trying to take control through aggression.

You may have heard the term 'toxic masculinity', as it has been used a lot in the media recently, but do you know where it came from? It arose out of a men's movement in the 1980s and was aimed at removing 'limiting male stereotypes' (males as 'warriors' or 'kings'). In other words, the phrase was used to identify behaviours that were toxic to men, such as avoiding expressing emotions, shame, extreme self-reliance, extreme desires to dominate, putting down anything perceived as feminine in another male, or devaluing women. [7]

The problem is that in recent times this term has been misused to infer that all aspects of masculinity are bad and toxic to women. This misuse has made it seem like masculinity is pathological, and this has caused controversy and a sense of 'attack' on men. Masculinity does *not* equal 'toxic masculinity'. What the term intends to convey is that living up to rigid stereotypes about what it is to be male has contributed to many mental health issues, as well as to problems in the community such as domestic violence.

With all of this discussion in the community and media about masculinity, some men will have felt liberated, but others may have felt confused about their identity. We all need a sense of self, and it is stressful if the identity you have developed is challenged or threatened. We need to allow for differences among both men and women, as we all have different strengths, personalities and life experiences.

For all of these reasons, there is a need to explore new values for men and to take a stand against any damaging ideas about masculinity in our society. It is also vital to take a stand against unacceptable behaviours by anyone, whether that involves emotional, sexual or physical violence.

SHAME

Shame is a huge barrier to acknowledging there is a mental health issue and getting help. Author Tim Grayburn has written about how depression and anxiety impacted his life. He was reluctant to tell his family or partner about feeling anxious and depressed for many years because of a sense of shame. Tim has described the sense of fear that comes with a diagnosis of depression and that upon seeing a doctor and discussing the diagnosis, he had 'images of being tied up in some dungeon'. He felt disappointed in himself, ostracized and 'broken'.[8] Tim went on to find ways to manage his anxiety and depression and is sharing his knowledge by writing and speaking about his experience.

Let's look at shame in more detail. Brené Brown started researching men and shame after speaking at a book launch about her research into women and shame. A man in the audience came up to her afterwards and asked why she did not do research about men. He said that his family would prefer to see him 'die on top of [his] white horse, rather than see [him] fall off it'. This triggered her to begin to talk to men about shame.

Brown asked men what shame meant to them, and they responded with a 'failure [whether] at work, on the sporting field, in marriage or in bed'. It meant 'being wrong or defective in some way'. It also meant 'showing fear' or other people thinking you are 'soft', which was thought of as being degrading.[9]

Brown writes about how people need a sense of love and belonging and need to be part of something that gives their lives meaning. We try to fit in and do what society (or marketing) tells us to do — not to be 'weak', to work out, buy cool clothes or do a certain job. It is extremely painful when we think we don't fit in or are not worthy in some way.

Brown has developed useful definitions of two common

feelings, namely shame and guilt. The difference is important as they are associated with different outcomes. Shame is related to depression and suicide, addictions and violence, whereas guilt is not. Shame involves a focus on self, with thoughts like 'I am bad' or 'I am a mistake', meaning that there is something 'inherently wrong with who I am'. Guilt relates to behaviours or actions, with related thoughts such as 'I did something bad' or 'I made a mistake'.

KEY POINT

Men are being socialized to project being great and powerful, no matter how they feel or how hard they are working on the inside. The push to 'be a man' is full of 'shoulds' and can amplify shame if you sense you are lacking in manliness in any way. In addition, women can struggle to deal with men expressing their vulnerability as they too are socialized to expect a man to be 'strong' and riding high on that white horse!

Men naturally want to be 'one of the boys' and they innately measure up to other males. The trap here is thinking you are 'not good enough'. This can lead to a sense of being disconnected from yourself, feeling insecure, setting unrealistic expectations, feeling numb, or it can result in aggression. Experiences of shame in childhood can lead to being self-critical and an inner voice can develop saying 'you are weak or useless'.

Think about the statement 'to man up'. It implies being tough and hard. But what if men incorporated what society sees as 'soft' qualities as well, such as being sensitive or kind? These characteristics may have negative connotations for men in our society, but 'soft' does not mean an absence of courage. It actually means being flexible, compassionate and courageous. [10]

WHAT WE HAVE LOOKED AT SO FAR!

At the centre of men's mental health issues is understanding masculinity in our society, and the expectations that are placed on men. We know that living up to rigid traditional stereotypes about what it is to be male have contributed to many mental health issues.

Stigma about mental health in the community is a barrier to seeking help. Olympic swimmer Ian Thorpe was asked, 'If you could change anything from the past 30 years, what would it be?' He answered, 'I wish we had started the conversation around mental health earlier and removed the ... stigma that has long been associated with it. Personally, I wish I believed earlier on that my struggles were manageable with the right treatment and then I may not have been to the dark places I have been. I also would have tried not to be so hard on myself.'[11]

Shame can result when men sense they don't measure up to expectations, but it is often a hidden emotion. It is also the one most likely to motivate men to stay away from the help they need. Shame is behind the scenes with problems like performance anxiety, eating disorders and addictions. Being open to shame means being vulnerable. This does not mean weakness or lack of masculinity. It can be an act of courage and can deepen our connection to others.

Researchers in the field of shame have provided some potential answers, such as being aware of the issues, working through shame rather than avoiding it, developing more understanding of emotions, developing empathy and working with thoughts. We will address all of these in this book.

....

KEY POINTS

WHAT YOU NEED TO KNOW ABOUT MEN'S MENTAL HEALTH

- Caring for your mental health is one of the keys to feeling healthy and happy.
- You need to address the basic needs in life, as well as your psychological needs and your need to 'belong'.
- Focus on all aspects of your wellbeing; that is, your physical health, your emotions and your relationships.
- Society has definite ideas about what it is to be a 'man'. Some of these ideas cause harm and distress and need to be challenged. It is not 'soft' to express your feelings, to be kind or to feel vulnerable.
- Men experience a whole range of mental health issues and many do not seek help. It can appear 'weak' to ask for some help, but it actually takes courage.
- Suicide rates in men are way too high. This is a crisis we mustn't ignore.

2.

TWELVE KEY TOOLS TO IMPROVE YOUR MENTAL HEALTH

Everything can be taken from a man but one thing: the last of human freedoms — to choose one's attitude in any given set of circumstances, to choose one's own way.

Viktor Frankl

There is a lot to learn about your mental health and how to tackle any troublesome issues. The twelve key tools outlined in this chapter will enable you to work on mental health issues. There is no specific order in which to use the tools, as different men will have different needs. For some, seeking help might come first, while for others, improving lifestyle is a priority. However, each tool will guide you to addressing any mental health issue in a positive way.

THE TWELVE KEY TOOLS

The twelve key tools are part of a toolkit that will help you identify and focus on any mental health issue you may be experiencing. The tools are drawn from current approaches and from many years of experience working with men. They are designed to address all aspects of yourself and your life to ensure the best recovery possible. The twelve key tools are:

1. Identify the key issue(s).
2. Set some goals.
3. See your doctor and have a check-up.
4. Focus on your lifestyle.
5. Gather information about your issue(s).
6. Reach out to others.
7. Consider counselling or talking therapies.
8. Utilize your work and other meaningful activities.
9. Consider complementary therapies.
10. Work on prevention.
11. Consider whether medication has a role.
12. Practice and more practice!

You may find these tools useful and decide to adopt some or all of them.

1. Identify the key issue(s)

To assist you to identify some of the key factors or issues related to your mental health, here are some questions to ask yourself. Try to answer them honestly:

1. Are any physical factors contributing to your mental health (e.g. being exhausted, not sleeping or eating well, drug use or chronic illness)?
2. Are any emotional factors contributing to your mental health (e.g. grief, trauma, shame, anger, feeling anxious or depressed)?

3. Are any social issues affecting your mental health (e.g. being homeless or unemployed, worrying about money or sex, relationship difficulties)?
4. Do you feel stress or dissatisfaction at work? Are you getting some time off to do the activities that you enjoy?
5. Do you have any spiritual concerns, such as questions about what life is about?
6. Are any cultural factors affecting your mental health?
7. Do you have any sexuality or gender-related issues?

Did you learn more about yourself or identify any significant issues by answering these questions? If you are struggling to know what the main issues are, here is a helpful exercise to assist. It involves looking at your values and seeing where things may be lacking. The main areas in life (relationships, work, leisure) are listed in the left-hand column of the table. In relation to each of these areas, ask yourself the following questions:

- What is important to you or what do you value in each life area? Write your answers in the first column (complete this first).
- Is there a gap between what is important, and what is actually happening at the moment in this area? Write down your thoughts in the second column.
- And then consider: What issues or feelings are arising as a result of this gap? Jot your thoughts down in the third column.

EXPLORING YOUR VALUES

Life areas	What is important to you in this area?	Is there a gap between what is important and what is happening at the moment?	What issues are arising from this gap?
Example: Health and wellbeing	*Being fit and healthy*	*Yes, not doing any exercise*	*Feeling tired and depressed*
Health and wellbeing			
Family and friends			
Partner relationships			
Work/ finances			
Education/ self-development			
Leisure			

EXPLORING YOUR VALUES

Life areas	What is important to you in this area?	Is there a gap between what is important and what is happening at the moment?	What issues are arising from this gap?
Community			
Environment			
Spirituality			

The exercise helps you to identify your values, and these are central to your happiness and leading a fulfilling life. It also highlights potential gaps, which may be leading to distressing feelings or issues needing some work. Here's an example of how useful this exercise can be:

A young man called Tim, who was in his early twenties, went to see his doctor. He was struggling with gambling and drug use. It was doing the values exercise that enabled Tim to understand the various social issues he had that he could finally talk about. Anxiety in social situations, along with feeling a need to be

accepted by his mates, were significant issues. Tim had started
using drugs to cope with the anxiety.

2. Set some goals

Now that you have identified some relevant issues (e.g. feeling
anxious or depressed, struggling with poor sleep, lack of exercise,
work stress or addiction), another useful tool can be setting some
goals to help address these issues.

Remember that you intuitively know how to set a goal but
taking the first step can often be the hardest part. For example,
you may put off a particular task for a while, but once you decide
and do some planning, you may find it easier to manage than
expected! Here are some tips for goal-setting:

- Goals need to be specific, your own, and achievable or realistic.
- To help with motivation, it's good to think about *why* you want to work towards the goal or consider the benefits. (Also check out how to build motivation in Chapter 5.)
- You may want to start with one goal, so you don't feel overwhelmed.
- It's best to work towards goals in a series of small steps (achieving a step spurs you on to the next one).
- Set a timeframe for starting (e.g. next Monday), and consider when you want to achieve the goal by.

TIP: Always plan small steps when setting goals. Sometimes the first step is the hardest, but once you have taken that first one, the others often follow. Then keep stepping!

Here is an example:

My goal = to do more exercise and get out into nature by walking along a (particular) hiking trail near the coast.

Steps to achieve my goal:
1. *Put details into my GPS and work out how far away it is.*
2. *Work out when to go and who to go with.*
3. *Decide whether to go for a day or weekend.*
4. *Buy supplies (food, fuel).*
5. *Take some photos on the walk.*

Why? It will be good to get some exercise and check out the ocean.

Date to achieve this goal by? Saturday.

Now have a go at writing down one of your goals (and you might like to copy this template to enable you to work on more goals later on):

SETTING GOALS
My goal =

Steps to achieve my goal:
1.
2.
3.
4.
5.

Why do I want to achieve this goal (the benefits)?:

Date for starting:

I will know I have achieved it when:

Date to achieve my goal by:

3. See your doctor and have a check-up

Your physical health is central to enjoying life. It's also important to make sure that there are no underlying physical issues which might be triggering problems with your mental health. This is why seeing a doctor for a check-up is recommended.

Men, as well as women, need regular physical and mental health checks. Your doctor can talk to you about your health, any family history of illnesses and your lifestyle. They can work through any current issues, such as injuries, tiredness or sexual problems, and check up on your mood, sleep or related issues.

A doctor can carry out any relevant health checks such as blood pressure, and do a general physical examination and some investigations if needed. Depending on your age or history, some screening tests may be suggested (blood sugar level tests, electrocardiograph, prostate, bone or bowel health tests). Sometimes health problems such as anaemia, low vitamin D or thyroid issues can trigger emotional issues, and improvements can be felt when these are treated. Chronic illnesses, such as diabetes, or conditions such as Parkinson's disease or sleep apnoea may greatly impact your mental health.

Some men may feel reluctant to approach a doctor about health issues, or to ask about particular ailments due to embarrassment (e.g. prostate health, erectile dysfunction). But these sorts of problems are common, and doctors are used to talking about them. So whether you are a young or older man, it's *okay* to raise any issues (including mental health issues) that you are concerned about or want checked out.

TIP: See your doctor and have a talk and a check-up. Why not go soon or set a goal to see your doctor at least once a year? Make a list of your concerns and questions and take it with you so they can be addressed.

---

4. Focus on your lifestyle

Lifestyle is a broad term and includes your nutrition, sleep, physical fitness and taking time out to relax. Don't underestimate the importance of lifestyle. Remember that an athlete who doesn't eat well, drink plenty of water, get regular sleep and train regularly, will not perform well when they compete. In the same way, your physical and mental health will suffer if you don't pay attention to your lifestyle.

We have seen individuals make a big difference to their mental health by improving their lifestyle:

Corey, who was feeling very anxious, was drinking 2 litres (4¼ pints) of caffeinated soft drinks a day. He felt less anxious after switching to water.

Harry was feeling down and had not been seeing much sunlight due to shift work. He was found to be low in vitamin D, and eating more fish, taking some vitamin D supplements and getting some daily sunshine helped lift his mood.

The following exercise allows you to answer some questions about different aspects of your lifestyle and whether they may be contributing to your mental health. Look at each one and tick 'yes' or 'no'.

TAKING A LOOK AT YOUR LIFESTYLE

Questions	Yes	No
• Do you regularly socialize with friends and family? Or connect with people?		

TAKING A LOOK AT YOUR LIFESTYLE

Questions	Yes	No
• Are you making sure that you regularly eat fresh and healthy foods?		
• What is your weight like? Do you think it is fairly healthy?		
• Do you drink plenty of water?		
• Do you keep caffeinated drinks (coffee, tea, cola) to a minimum?		
• If you drink alcohol, do you mostly stick to one or two standard drinks, rather than more?		
• Do you have a couple of alcohol-free days each week?		
• Are you a non-smoker?		
• Do you avoid using recreational drugs, or keep use to a minimum?		
• Do you get some regular exercise?		
• Is your sex life satisfactory?		
• Do you sleep well and feel rested when you wake up?		
• Do you make sure that you spend time away from technology each day?		
• Do you have some silent time each day?		
• Do you make time to reflect on life?		
• Are you aware of when you are stressed and take measures to reduce your stress levels (e.g. exercise, talking to friends/family, listening to music)?		
• Do you regularly take time out to unwind and relax?		
• Do you spend time with pets?		
• Do you declutter your room/house/wardrobe from time to time?		

TAKING A LOOK AT YOUR LIFESTYLE		
Questions	**Yes**	**No**
• Do you have some mini-breaks away or take a holiday regularly?		
• Are you exposed to a reasonable amount of sunshine each day?		
• Do you laugh regularly?		

How many 'yes' and 'no' responses did you have? Congratulations on the 'yes' responses; the more the better. And maybe the 'no's' need some attention!

REVAMPING YOUR LIFESTYLE

- Think about ways to connect with other people (e.g. family and friends, work colleagues or join a group!)
- Your body and brain require good nutrition. This means eating a variety of foods, including proteins (meat or fish, or various nuts and beans if vegetarian or vegan). Make sure to include plenty of fresh fruit and vegetables, as well as dairy products (unless you have intolerances) to get the nutrition you need.
- Shop around the edges of the supermarket where all the fresh food is or try farmer's markets for a change.
- Omega-3 oils (found in nuts and fish) are important for brain function. And vitamins B12 and B9 (active folate) have also been found to assist mood. Include foods rich in these nutrients (legumes, green vegetables) or think about whether supplements might help.

- Work on your weight if you are not comfortable with it, or if your weight is impacting your wellbeing. You may choose to see a nutritionist, practise eating in a mindful way, or tackle emotional eating.
- Drink at least 2 litres (4¼ pints) of water a day. Consider whether you need to have fewer caffeinated or energy drinks, as they can creep up in number.
- Follow the guidelines for alcohol as much as you can. If you do drink, aim to keep to two drinks a day, and have several alcohol-free days each week.
- Look at ways to quit smoking (e.g. going cold turkey, cutting down, medications or hypnosis). Smoking is a habit, and there are often triggers or associations to having a cigarette such as first thing in the morning, with a coffee, on a break from work or after meals. Changing the way you do things (e.g. having water instead of a hot drink), or going for a walk instead of standing with smokers, can assist.
- Work on reducing the use of other substances, and get some help if need be (see Chapter 5 on substance-related issues).
- Get some regular exercise, aiming for at least 30 minutes every day, and walk to the shops instead of driving, or take the stairs at work.
- Having a satisfying sexual relationship can influence your emotional wellbeing. Your sex life will vary at different times, but feeling good about yourself, your sexuality and your relationships are key.

- If sleep is an issue, work on ways to improve it. Avoid caffeine, go to bed at a regular time, wind down beforehand, get off screens, and make sure your bedroom is quiet and comfortable. This is called 'good sleep hygiene' and it can be very effective (more on this on page 100).
- Have sleep apnoea checked out if you don't wake up rested, struggle with snoring, fall asleep during the day or your partner tells you that you stop breathing at night.
- Don't forget to disconnect from your phone, tablet or laptop regularly. Our brain needs time away from being stimulated by technology, and it needs silence too. (More on the impact of technology later.)
- Do more of the activities that you enjoy and find meaningful. What did you enjoy when you were young? Sometimes these activities can still be very enjoyable as adults.
- Find time to relax. Some people find music or exercise relaxing, while others find using a relaxation app helpful. Perhaps learn to meditate or try yoga.
- Learn about 'mindfulness', and practise mindfulness in everyday activities, or mindfulness meditation (covered in detail in the next chapter).
- Get out into nature regularly (e.g. walk barefoot on the beach, surf or walk in the forest).
- Have a laugh as humour de-stresses you.

Another interesting concept related to lifestyle is 'work–life integration', which fits well with the 'whole person' approach, as it is about looking at all areas of life, prioritizing your different needs, and looking for ways to blend different areas of life to improve your wellbeing. Here are some examples. If you catch the train to work, walking to and from the station each day could provide some regular exercise. Having boundaries about not checking any emails after the end of the formal workday enables you to enjoy time to relax on your own, or spend time with a partner or family.

5. Gather information about your issue(s)

Having information aids your understanding of emotional health and empowers you to make some changes in life. That is what this book is all about. You may also gather information by talking to people, including those who have had similar life experiences as you, or various professionals.

Other sources of information might be the radio or podcasts, going online or via apps. Make sure you are looking at websites that are well researched and written. Good advice has good evidence behind it, so learn to recognize quality sources of information (see also the Resources section at the end of this book).

6. Reach out to others

Men tend to keep their worries and feelings to themselves but, in our experience, this is gradually changing. Men are realizing that 'it's okay not to be okay,' and are beginning to ask more and more for help. In fact, talking with someone you trust, like a partner, family member or a trusted friend, can be really helpful.

Simply speaking out loud helps you express and work through your emotions. And it feels really good to be listened to and understood. These are basic human needs, so think about reaching out when the problem feels too big for you to carry on your own. You might also decide to reach out to a coach, work colleague, doctor or counsellor (see also the Resources section at the end of this book). Here is Jason's story:

> Jason, a 27-year-old graphic designer, was experiencing anxious feelings and low self-confidence, especially in relation to work. He had been having problems at work for several months, starting with the loss of a client. His two-year relationship had also broken down. His anxiety had been getting worse and he was waking up most nights with tight feelings in his abdomen and chest. He was beginning to doubt whether graphic design was for him!
>
> Jason decided to see a doctor, who did a physical check-up and also recommended Jason get back to exercising regularly and a more regular sleeping pattern. He suggested that Jason take a couple of days off work to get moving on these, and that he also consider seeing a therapist to talk about the life stress he was experiencing, the anxiety symptoms and his self-confidence.
>
> Jason felt more settled with these measures, and on his days off did some exercise, had better sleep and made an appointment to see a therapist.

7. Consider counselling or talking therapies

You may have heard about counselling or therapy. These practices are based on talking to someone who is trained and skilled, who can help you to understand yourself and what is going on in your life. Talking therapies help you reach into yourself and to tap into your own resources and address the issues. A therapist, such as a psychologist or other mental health professional, can help you to make changes in your thinking, feelings or actions. We will mostly use the term 'therapist' in this book.

Much humour has been generated over the years by the idea of being 'in therapy'. However, this humour relies on stereotypes that are not present in this book. The facts are that therapy is a widespread practice and that countless people have been helped by various forms of therapy. And there need be no stigma to the types of mainstream therapies talked about in this book.

TIP: If you seek out help from a therapist, make sure they have sound training, are professional in their approach, and that you feel comfortable talking with them. Your doctor can help you locate someone in your area and relevant professional organizations will have lists of trained therapists in your area.

Talking therapies have been influenced by our understanding of the nervous system, so we are going to take a quick look at the brain and how it controls the nervous system before looking at various therapies.

The brain is an amazing organ which carries out many functions, from helping our heart to beat, to making sense of what we see and hear. It allows us to relate to others and to come up with creative ideas. The areas of the brain of interest to us are:

- the brainstem at the top of the spinal cord, which controls basic functions of the body and is about survival

- the limbic brain (the amygdala and hippocampus), which is responsible for emotions and memory
- the cortex, which houses language, imagination and awareness, and is responsible for your decisions and judgement.

If you imagine a fist being like the brain, then the wrist and lower palm can represent the brainstem, the thumb is the limbic brain, and fingers are the cortex.

These three areas of the brain deal with several core human needs:

- To be safe = the brainstem.
- To feel satisfied or content = the limbic brain.
- To be connected with others = the cortex.[1]

What we know is that all parts of the brain and the rest of the nervous system are interconnected. We have a bias towards negative thinking to help us survive and be safe. Stress activates the brainstem and increases our heart and breathing rates as a survival response and any trauma is processed in the limbic brain. But most importantly, the brain is always changing, all through life, and this is how we learn!

KEY POINT

The reason that talking therapies help is that our brains can change, and as a result, we can learn. There are many tools to help with this process, and to help you deal with life events and with a range of issues related to thoughts and feelings.

Talking therapies help our brain to change the way we think and learn. A brief outline of some of the main talking therapies follows and they will be discussed further later in the book.

Cognitive behaviour therapy (CBT)

CBT is based on the idea that the way we think and what we do influence how we feel. In fact, they all influence each other, as do life situations, as shown in the following diagram:

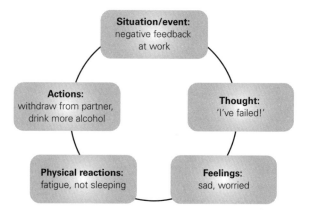

We all have self-talk or a constant stream of thoughts (about 60,000 a day, in fact), which can affect our feelings and actions. We often mix up feelings and thoughts, perhaps saying, 'I feel as though I've made a mess of everything.' This is actually a thought, and the related feeling might be disappointment. Some feelings or emotions seem more negative (e.g. fear or anger), but they exist to help us survive when we are in danger. The positive ones, such as happiness and joy, help us to achieve greater things in life. Cognitive behaviour therapy involves adopting helpful behaviours or actions (e.g. exercise, relaxation, doing hobbies), or working with any traps in our thinking. It helps you to recognize unhelpful thoughts, to challenge them, and to develop more helpful ways of thinking (more on this later).

Interpersonal therapy (IPT)

Based on the idea that emotional symptoms are connected to relationship distress, interpersonal therapy provides tools to improve symptoms and how you are functioning socially. It mostly focuses on the 'here and now', working on resolving relationship issues, and working with emotions. IPT identifies four common problem areas: grief due to loss; interpersonal disputes (conflict); role transitions or changes (such as beginning a job, getting married); and interpersonal sensitivities (e.g. having challenges with social situations or connecting to other people).

Mindfulness

Mindfulness means focusing on the present moment, on purpose and without judgement. For example, if you are eating a new delicious food, you are fully involved in using all of your senses, such as smell and taste, to enjoy it. Mindfulness is about keeping your head in the here and now, rather than in the past or future. You can practise being mindful through breathing exercises or meditation, or being in the moment when doing activities such as cooking or walking (everyday mindfulness). The reason mindfulness is so powerful is that when you are mindful, your brain cells actually grow. Being mindful also helps you to:

- enjoy the moment and relax
- be more connected to yourself and nature

- become more aware of thoughts and feelings and learn to relate to them differently
- be kinder to yourself (and that can be good!).

Acceptance and commitment therapy (ACT)

Based on the idea that you need to take action to change how you feel, ACT aims to help you become more flexible in your thinking, and to create a more meaningful life. It has six key processes:

1. Contact with the present moment = mindfulness.
2. Values = living according to what is important to you.
3. Committed action = no change happens without action.
4. Self-as-context = the ability of your mind to observe feelings and thoughts.
5. Defusion = detaching from or taking the power out of uncomfortable or unpleasant feelings and thoughts.
6. Acceptance = quit struggling with feelings that are uncomfortable and focus on what you can control in the situation.

8. Utilize your work and other meaningful activities

Life is all about activity. Our daily routine, work and leisure all involve a range of activities. They foster a sense of meaning and purpose, provide us with routine and enjoyment in life, and can give us a great sense of satisfaction and achievement.

Loss of motivation or lethargy are common when issues with mental health are pushing you around, which means that you may find it harder to do the activities that usually provide you with pleasure or satisfaction.

Different individuals enjoy different sorts of activities. Some people enjoy movement (sport, walking the dog), while others relate to music or visual activities (watching films, drawing). Some activities are very social (team sports, joining a running group), while some have physical health benefits or incorporate relaxation (yoga). Creative pursuits, such as music or carpentry, allow you to express yourself and build self-confidence.

Activities that involve helping others or teaching a skill can be especially rewarding. Caring for a pet may also give you a great deal of pleasure.

Men's lives can be greatly changed through activity:

Wayne, a retired 64 year old, had experienced anxiety and depression at different times in his life. He discovered that his wellbeing very much depended on being involved with other people and doing activities that he enjoyed. He learnt wood-turning and joined a local group of wood-turners. He attended classes at the local gym and also walked his dog Jasper every day on the beach.

The key is finding activities that are meaningful to you personally (we will look at this more in later chapters).

9. Consider complementary therapies

You may want to look at complementary therapies. Here are some thoughts about them.

Approaches such as massage or herbal medication may be useful to help deal with mental health issues. Various herbal medicines or supplements are used for mild depression and anxiety, such as St John's Wort (hypericum) and SAMe (S-adenosyl methionine).

It is often presumed complementary treatments are fully safe, but there may be potential risks. Herbal medicines or supplements can have side effects and interactions with other medicines, so always discuss this with a qualified healthcare practitioner before taking any complementary medicines, and always let your doctor know about what you are taking. Complementary approaches and prescribed treatments can work well together.

10. Work on prevention

This book is not just about working on your current mental health, but also on preventing issues from arising or from recurring in the future. In general, prevention is about:

- reducing any risk factors, such as poor nutrition, substance use, stress, trauma or social isolation, and
- improving some of the protective factors such as healthy lifestyle, connecting with others and doing meaningful activities in life.

A specific approach that is helpful in terms of prevention is 'positive psychology'. Developed by Martin Seligman, positive psychology focuses on character strengths and behaviours, and aims to help people achieve their optimal health and wellbeing (see Resources section at the end of the book). Positive psychology achieves this by focusing on PERMA:

- Positive emotions (such as joy or love).
- Engagement in life and activities.
- Relationships.

- Meaning in life.
- Accomplishment.

A therapy called 'positive therapy' has come out of PERMA, involving:

- Identifying strengths and encouraging more use of them.
- Tapping into positive emotions (e.g. gratitude and kindness).
- Connecting with others (e.g. talking with friends, reaching out to other men).
- Enjoying leisure and creativity.
- Engaging in life and being in 'flow' (feeling in the zone when doing something you really enjoy).
- Developing skills for healthy relationships.
- Utilizing mindfulness, self-care and positive coping skills.
- Considering the role of values and being your authentic self.
- Fostering accomplishment, a sense of purpose, meaning and hope.
- Building resilience skills and flourishing in life.

We have already touched on some of these points and you will find a number of tools in this book are drawn from positive therapy. Let's focus on one right now, namely, identifying and using your strengths. We know that people who recognize and work with their strengths tend to be happier and less stressed. Society tends to hold ideas about what male strengths should be (e.g. strong and successful) and growing up in our society influences you to take on these ideas. But some of these ideas are not always helpful. Remember that strengths can be remarkably broad and include assets such as creativity and kindness.

Complete the following exercise, as the knowledge that it gives you will become a valuable tool in helping you focus more on your strengths and assets each day. In this way you will improve your mental health and wellbeing.

DISCOVER YOUR STRENGTHS, THEN USE THEM EVERY DAY!

Take some time to get to know your strengths in more detail. Start by making a list of them. Examples can include being kind, caring, considerate, reliable, punctual, active, resourceful, artistic, creative, musical, organized, a good listener, witty, adventurous, friendly, outgoing, environmentally conscious, an animal-lover, a good cook, a good friend, determined or hard-working.

If you struggle with this, ask a trusted family member or friend what they think, or you can do a strengths questionnaire at www.authentichappiness.sas.upenn.edu.

Let's also come back to the idea that people seem to more easily recognize the need to look after their physical health rather than their mental health. Research has found that we instinctively know what helps our mental health, but often disregard this 'intuition'.[2]

Intuition refers to your instinctive knowledge or what you know without knowing how you know! For example, you may have worked out that getting enough sleep, doing regular exercise, eating fresh food, spending time with friends or heading to the beach helps you feel good.

TAP INTO YOUR INTUITION

Take another moment to think about what you know about the sort of endeavours that help your mental health. Make a list, then do more of the things on your list!

We could talk about prevention for a lot longer, and we'll come back to it in Chapter 11.

11. Consider whether medication has a role

A range of medications are used in treating issues such as depression and other mood disorders, as well as anxiety and schizophrenia. However, the word 'medication' itself usually provokes anxiety! The decision as to whether or not to consider medication often comes down to how severe the mental health issue is and how much it is stopping you from functioning in your life. Usually the talking therapies are tapped into first, but sometimes there will be such a lot of suffering that we start to think about whether medication might help.

Men may be reluctant to consider medication, often because of misinformation or bias in the community. Keeping an open mind is helpful, as is the doctor providing information about the various types of medication, their use and potential side effects. Rather than dismissing the idea, an option is to put the idea on a 'shelf' in your mind for a while and come back to it later to consider it again.

We are not going to discuss medication in detail, as it is best to talk to your doctor about it, but here are some guidelines:

- When there are very troublesome issues with mental health (e.g. moderate or severe symptoms of depression), there may be a place for medication.
- However, make sure a 'whole person' approach is being taken. In general, start with information, addressing lifestyle and utilizing talking therapies.
- When there are significant symptoms, including suicidal thoughts, make sure you seek help from your doctor. You can work together to assess what support is needed and can decide together if medication may help recovery.
- Medication should not be the only treatment. Better long-term outcomes occur when talking therapies are also used.

12. Practice and more practice!

With learning any new skill in life (e.g. a sport, mechanics or a musical instrument), you have to take action and practise. It's the same with improving your mental health — it takes reading and re-reading to understand the concepts and putting the various ideas and tools into practice regularly. In the same way that you go to the gym to work out, you can see this effort with your mental health as a workout!

The reason that practice works is that you are putting in effort mindfully. This means that the brain is actually laying down new neural pathways (rewiring) and gradually changing your way of thinking or behaving. The new nerve cells actually grow and link up, and you get better at whatever you are practising. This makes sense when you think about the different things you have practised and mastered in the past (e.g. kicking a football or playing a computer game).

UNDERSTANDING HOW YOUR BRAIN CHANGES WITH PRACTICE

Firstly, write your name with your dominant hand, then swap the pen to your other hand and write your name again. Notice how much harder this is! If you want to learn to write with your non-dominant hand you can, by practising, and over time your brain will rewire itself. A YouTube clip by Dr Joe Despenza called 'Look what happens in your brain when you change your mind' shows this phenomenon really well.

So, there are good reasons to keep reading, and gradually put some of the ideas into practice. And then keep practising some more!

WHAT WE HAVE LOOKED AT SO FAR!

Having read about the twelve key tools, take a few moments to reflect on which ones seem most useful for you. Now is the time to take some small steps in relation to your mental health and wellbeing by putting some of the tools into action.

But before moving on to the next chapter, you might like to complete the Kessler Psychological Distress Scale or K10 questionnaire below (see also the Resources section at the end of the book). Developed in the United States and used worldwide, it is a measure of current psychological distress but does not diagnose particular problems. A high score, however, can indicate that there could be issues such as anxiety or depression that need to be checked out further with a health professional.

KESSLER PSYCHOLOGICAL DISTRESS SCALE (K10)

Think about the past four weeks, then answer each question by choosing the number on the scale that seems to fit.

Scale:
1 = none of the time
2 = a little of the time
3 = some of the time
4 = most of the time
5 = all of the time

Questions:
   1. About how often did you feel tired out for no good reason? (Scale number =) _____
   2. About how often did you feel nervous? _____
   3. About how often did you feel so nervous that nothing could calm you down? _____

4. About how often did you feel hopeless? _____
5. About how often did you feel restless or fidgety? _____
6. About how often did you feel so restless that you could not sit still? _____
7. About how often did you feel depressed? _____
8. About how often did you feel that everything was an effort? ___
9. About how often did you feel so sad that nothing could cheer you up? _____
10. About how often did you feel worthless? _____

Now, add up the numbers to give a total score out of 50. If the score is:
- less than 20, there is no distress
- between 20 and 24, there is mild distress
- between 25 and 29, there is moderate distress
- more than 30, there is severe distress.

If the score is above 20, and especially above 25, please think about seeing a doctor or therapist, in addition to working through this book.

3.

TACKLING STRESS
AND ANXIETY

Not until we are lost do we begin to understand ourselves.
Henry David Thoreau

Stress and anxiety are part of life, but they can be tough to handle when they are extreme. The more you know about stress and anxiety, and the more tools you have to manage them, the less power they will have in your life. Let's define them first:

Stress comes from demands on you, whether it's by earning money, finding time to get to the gym, or meeting the needs of partners or family.

Anxiety is a normal feeling, and everyone experiences it. It is related to fear, and you may be aware of it in situations that are very stressful, or where there is some perceived 'threat', such as going to a job interview or being in trouble in some way.

Feeling some stress or anxiety can actually help you to perform better (e.g. in a football match or an exam), but when there is too much of it, your performance can be affected. An example is a student studying hard and knowing their work, but in the exam their mind goes 'blank' due to a surge of anxiety.

This chapter describes practical tools that can help with stress and anxiety. They may also be helpful with some other mental health issues. Take your time to read about them and to try them out to see what you want to include in your toolkit.

UNDERSTANDING STRESS AND ANXIETY

Anxiety can help you survive when you are in danger but, in many cases, anxiety can feel awful, and can interfere with your life, relationships or work. Here are some facts about anxiety:

- Anxiety is often about something that might happen in the future, such as feeling anxious before giving a talk or asking someone out.
- You can recognize when you are feeling anxious by what you experience in your body and mind. You might have racing thoughts, a feeling of dread, sweating, feeling tension in your muscles, or notice that your heart is beating fast in your chest or that your breathing is fast and shallow.
- You might also notice more frequent headaches, being grumpy or angry, finding it hard to get off to sleep, having broken sleep or having a lowered sex drive.

KEY POINT

Feeling stressed or anxious is NOT a sign of weakness, but a part of life.

Experiencing stress or anxiety is very different from having an anxiety disorder. When anxiety is severe, or it persists and impacts your ability to function, it might fit with a disorder. Anxiety disorders are very common in the community. Men are about half as likely as women to experience an anxiety disorder during their lives. Men often seek help for anxiety later than women and are more likely to use substances like alcohol or drugs to deal with the symptoms. Having an anxiety disorder also means that you are more at risk of depression. There are different kinds of anxiety disorders, such as:

- Phobias or specific fears (e.g. fear of heights or snakes).
- Social anxiety (fear of embarrassment in social situations or being thought of negatively by others).
- Panic disorder (repeated 'panic attacks' or episodes of severe anxiety).
- Agoraphobia (fear of not being able to escape or of open spaces).
- Generalized anxiety (worrying most of the time about a range of issues).
- Obsessive-compulsive disorder (ruminating about things that might harm you or others and carrying out repeated behaviours to relieve that worry e.g. checking or washing hands).

Anxiety can also occur as part of depression or may be the effect of some substances. Some anxiety is associated with feeling disconnected or dissociated from a situation (e.g. feeling separate from your body and like you are looking on to the situation).

Post-traumatic stress disorder, which can follow traumatic events, can trigger anxiety symptoms, such as panic episodes, irritability, feeling on high alert, flashbacks to the traumatic situation, and disturbed sleep, often due to nightmares. We will cover this in Chapter 7.

A common question is: *What causes anxiety?* There are various ideas about this. We know that the stress response is 'hardwired' in our nervous system to protect us. This means the response is automatic when we are under threat. We also know that certain chemicals in the body (brain chemicals, hormones) are involved when there is anxiety. The following list outlines factors which can play a role in causing or worsening anxiety:

- Some health issues and drugs.
- Some families are more prone to anxiety; that is, there can be a genetic predisposition for anxiety.
- The level of anxiety can depend on the level of life stress. Having a number of causes of stress (e.g. financial, health, relationship issues) can worsen the anxiety.
- Some people have personality traits that can contribute to anxiety. Examples are being a perfectionist or being more obsessive than others.
- How you think can influence anxiety. Men who are more pessimistic may be more prone to anxiety, or those who think they always need to be in control.
- Your level of anxiety can also relate to what your coping skills are like in life. If you are good at problem-solving, you tend to move into this when faced with an issue, rather than worrying about it. Or a coping skill might be recognizing that it is important to relax after work, rather than thinking all evening about work.
- Social disadvantage can contribute to experiencing anxiety (e.g. inadequate housing, clothing or food).

- Anxiety can also be related to how you have been raised. Anxiety will be more likely if you have experienced neglect or any of the forms of abuse (e.g. being put down constantly or experiencing physical or sexual abuse).
- Trauma can trigger anxiety. Trauma may be obvious, such as a car accident or being assaulted, but it may not be so obvious. It can arise at school from a teacher who yells constantly or slams the desk unexpectedly, or from bullying by other students.
- Social isolation can be a cause. We feel happier and more relaxed when we connect with people and have some support.
- Spiritual triggers can also occur, such as issues within a church or your own personal struggles with your beliefs.

KEY POINT

There are many potential causes and triggers for anxiety, ranging from physical health issues to trauma or being isolated socially.

WAYS TO REDUCE STRESS AND ANXIETY

There are many ways to reduce stress and anxiety. The ideas in this chapter come from a number of psychological approaches that we introduced in the last chapter, and lots of experience. Use your own judgement as you read through them and try out the various exercises. See which ones work best for you, put them in your toolkit, and use them regularly.

Understand how the body responds to stress and anxiety

Knowledge empowers you and relieves worry, so let's explore how the nervous system and your body respond to a threat. You might have heard of the 'fight–flight–freeze response'. The limbic brain and brainstem, working closely with the body, are responsible for this response.

In 'caveman' times, when out hunting for food, men might have come face to face with a dangerous animal. They would have seen the animal, their brain would have recognized the danger, and then a number of changes would have happened in the body to prepare them to either fight or run back to the cave!

This response is still 'hardwired' into men's brains today. When it occurs, the body releases a lot of stress hormones (cortisol, adrenaline and norepinephrine). The same changes can happen in your body today when faced with any threat:

- Your heart rate increases to pump blood to the muscles (to prepare you to run or fight) and away from the brain, the skin, the fingers and toes, and the gut. You don't need to digest food if you are about to be eaten!
- Glucose moves into the bloodstream to provide energy.
- You become more alert through the senses (hearing, sight, smell).
- You sweat more to cool the body.
- Your breathing rate increases to get more oxygen around the body.

Sometimes you might also respond by freezing — this is being very still, almost like 'playing dead', in an attempt to avoid the threat. Here is the story of Simon to illustrate how the anxiety response can help:

Simon, a 37-year-old optometrist, had been experiencing worrying symptoms including palpitations and dizziness. He found that he could not think at work when the symptoms came on. He went to see his doctor to seek out the cause of the symptoms.

The doctor spoke with Simon and found that Simon had recently started his own business, and this had been a very stressful time. The doctor did some checks and was able to explain to him that anxiety was causing the symptoms. He also explained the 'fight or flight' response and what was occurring in his body. This explanation, along with doing some breathing exercises, helped Simon settle the anxiety.

It is important to understand that the fight–flight–freeze response is actually there to protect you. The changes in the body generally won't harm you, but they don't feel good either. They are not a sign you are 'going crazy', but they are a sign of stress or anxiety. In the modern world, the threat may no longer be a wild animal, but it could be an upsetting social media post, a job loss, a financial problem or a relationship issue.

Focus on a healthy lifestyle

Focusing on a healthy lifestyle is important in reducing stress and anxiety. You might like to go back and look at the tips on revamping your lifestyle on pages 26–27, however the following ones are particularly relevant for coping with anxiety. Consider which ones you might take on board in your life and make a note:

- Limit alcohol and caffeine.
- Get some regular exercise.
- If sleep is an issue, work on ways to improve it (see page 100).

- Do more of the activities you enjoy and connect with others.
- Take time out to relax (e.g. get out into nature or meditate).
- Practise mindfulness often.
- Disconnect from your phone, tablet or laptop regularly.

Talk with someone you trust, plus have a check-up

It is good to reach out and talk to someone you trust. This may be family or friends. Sharing a worry can help reduce it. And if you are concerned about the level of stress or anxiety that you are feeling and perhaps the associated physical symptoms, it can be helpful to see a doctor.

Find a doctor you are comfortable with. You can talk with them, and they may do a physical check-up to make sure there are no physical health issues involved. If relevant, the doctor can check for issues such as anaemia or an overactive thyroid, the symptoms of which can mimic anxiety.

A doctor can also listen and offer support, discuss your lifestyle and provide information. They can develop a thorough management plan with you, including what to do in a crisis. Some are trained in particular therapies, or they can suggest a therapist for you to see.

Reduce your 'stress bucket' and learn to relax

Each day is filled with demands, from getting up in the morning, to doing things for family members, going to work and paying bills. Imagine that you have a bucket inside of you. The bucket can hold a certain amount of stress or anxiety, but each demand made on you adds more to your stress bucket and it gradually fills up.

If the bucket gets too full, you might find that when a final stressful event happens (even a small thing), you 'spill over' or 'lose it' with feelings like irritability or frustration, and out-of-character behaviours. Have you ever experienced this?

GET TO KNOW YOUR STRESS BUCKET

It is important to look at what is going into your stress bucket. Are you expecting too much of yourself or taking on too much? Is work or home stressful, for example? Write some of your current stressors on the bucket. Then draw a line that shows how high your stress level is right now.

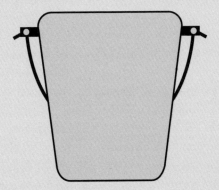

If your stress level is high, this is a good indication that you need to work on getting your stress level down, so keep reading!

The opposite of feeling stressed or anxious (and having an activated fight–flight–freeze response) is feeling chilled or relaxed, and so learning how to relax is vital in tackling stress and anxiety. Relaxation will lower the stress in your bucket!

We are going to take you through a range of ways to relax. Find what works best for you — it may be one of the suggestions, or it might be that physical exercise is right for you. But first, you need to understand something more about the two arms of our automatic or 'autonomic' nervous system — the sympathetic and parasympathetic nervous systems. The sympathetic nervous system fires up when you feel stress or anxiety and is responsible for the fight–flight–freeze response, while the parasympathetic nervous system is more active when we feel relaxed.

The easiest way to activate the parasympathetic system and to relax is to *breathe* effectively. This seems almost too simple, but it is true! This is why relaxation techniques and meditation often involve breathing exercises. Breathing actually calms the vagus nerve (part of the parasympathetic system) as it goes through your diaphragm (the muscle that divides the chest and the abdomen).

Start by getting to know the speed of your breathing rate.

KNOW YOUR BREATHING RATE

When you feel calm you take about 10 breaths per minute; however, during stress or anxiety you might take 25 breaths per minute. Take a moment to count your breaths for 30 seconds, then double the number to get your breathing rate. Is it more than 10 to 12? If so, then doing some breathing exercises will assist you.

Given that when feeling anxious, breathing is often faster and shallow, it is often very helpful to learn some breathing techniques. We have included a few for you to try now, but we encourage you to set aside time each day to practise them.

FIVE USEFUL BREATHING TECHNIQUES

1. Sit or stand up straight. Place your right hand on your upper chest and your left on your abdomen; take medium-sized breaths, focusing on breathing down into your abdomen. Feel the abdomen move out. Aim to breathe in for three counts and out for three counts — counting in, two, three and out, two, three — and this this will lead to you taking about ten breaths a minute. Once you have mastered this, try breathing out for a bit longer.

2. Breathe in and out through your nose if you are comfortable with this, or in through the nose and out through the mouth. Simply be aware of the breath in and then the breath out. Breathe at a gentle, slow pace, and feel the cooler air moving in. Breathe out and feel the warmer air moving out.

3. Count 'one' on your first breath in and 'one' on your first breath out, then 'two' on the next breath in and 'two' on the next breath out, and so on. Keep doing this until you reach ten, then start again at one.

4. Try 'box breathing'. Breath in slowly for four counts, hold your breath for four counts, breathe out for four counts, then hold again for four counts. Keep repeating these steps. Imagining the square shape of one side of a box can help.

5. Grab a piece of paper and a pen. Place a hand on the paper and slowly draw around your thumb, breathing in with the upstroke, and out with the downstroke. Repeat with each finger.

Physical relaxation is another great tool when you are wanting to feel more relaxed. You might find a massage relaxing or you can learn to relax your muscles by using 'progressive muscle relaxation'.

PROGRESSIVE MUSCLE RELAXATION

Sit down, make yourself comfortable and allow your eyes to close or focus on a spot in front of you. Be aware of your feet on the floor and your hands on your lap. Breathe gently in and out at a medium rate. As we go through the different parts of your body, notice how the muscles in that area are feeling. You may pick up some tightness or tension, but as you learn to let go of any tension in the muscles, they will loosen and feel more relaxed.

To begin, focus on the muscles in your face and notice how they feel. You might want to move them to get a sense of that. Then allow the muscles in your forehead to loosen and relax and then the muscles around your eyes, cheeks and jaw. Let your teeth sit a little apart.

Now allow your scalp to loosen and relax, then your neck muscles, particularly the muscles at the back of your neck. Let your shoulder muscles loosen and relax, then your upper arms, forearms and hands. Release any tension through your fingertips.

Be aware of your breath again, and the gentle movements of your chest with your breathing. Notice your chest muscles relaxing with every breath, feel your abdomen move with your breath, and relax. Allow your back muscles to relax from the top of the spine to the base of the spine, the buttock muscles relaxing too. Then allow relaxation to flow through your thighs, calves, and down into your feet and toes. Release any tension through your toes.

Enjoy these greater feelings of relaxation from head to toe for a few moments, then, when you are ready, have a gentle stretch and gradually open your eyes to bring your attention back to the room.

Other relaxation techniques include imagining a pleasant and safe place, such as a garden, park or a beach and spending time there in your mind doing what you want to do to relax and enjoy.

TIP: Try some breathing or meditation recordings. Some people find it easier to be guided through the techniques via a recording or app. Many are available, including free ones. (See the Resources section at the end of the book.)

Take some time to explore a few more ways you can tune in to being calmer in your life. You might like to use these relaxation techniques, or you may prefer to listen to music, read or watch a nature documentary. And to help get you into the habit of using your relaxation techniques or meditating regularly, consider keeping a diary for a week or so. It might look like this:

Relaxation diary		
	Type of relaxation (e.g. breathing, muscle relaxation, pleasant place, listening to music, meditation)	Record the time you spend relaxing (e.g. 10–10.30 a.m.)
Sunday		

Monday		
Tuesday		
Wednesday		
Thursday		
Friday		
Saturday		

Aim to do regular relaxation techniques or meditation. Remember, even a few minutes a day can be helpful. If you can do 15 to 20 minutes regularly, that is even better! By doing this your brain will gradually change and anxiety will lessen.

Ray, a 52-year-old man with arthritis and anxiety, took up yoga to aid his physical wellbeing. He found that he particularly enjoyed the meditation at the end of each session, finding that it enabled him to relax deeply. As a result, he began incorporating meditation into his life each day.

Identify some of the things causing stress and anxiety

Sometimes it helps to identify the issues in your life causing stress and anxiety, and actually write them down and get them out of your head onto paper. You also need to be aware of what is causing you distress before you can deal with the issues. So, take a few moments to step back and ask yourself what issues are causing you stress and anxiety:

- Are there 'external' causes, such as work, relationship problems or financial stress?
- Are there 'internal' ones, such as the demands you are putting on yourself?

MAKE A LIST OF TRIGGERS
Take a few moments to make a list of the main issues currently triggering stress and anxiety:

Men may be pushed around by the high expectations they put on themselves. Equally, some troublesome underlying or core beliefs can drive your anxious thoughts. These are beliefs formed in your mind as you grow up. You may not even be aware they are there and you tend to see them as true. Examples include: 'I must be 100 per cent in control at all times' or 'I must always be competent'. Remember that these are not actually possible! Or the thoughts may sound like: 'I am weak, not good enough, and unlovable' or 'something is wrong with me'. Remember, these are not based on truth!

And before you start thinking about how to tackle particular issues, look at this next exercise. It can actually take care of some of the issues you may have, and help you decide which ones to 'put the lid on' and which ones to focus on.

THREE LIFE BINS
There are three bins in life, each with a lid:
1. You and your goals, ideas and interests.
2. Other people.
3. The world you live in (politics, society, laws, environment, etc.).

You can lift the lid on the first bin and take a look inside at any time. You can spend a lot of time dealing with everything in this bin and have a lot of influence on it. With the second bin, you can help or hinder others, and influence this bin to some degree. Sometimes you need to put the lid on this bin and put it aside for a while. With the third bin, you can run for politics or plant trees, but again, there will be limits to what you can do.

The message is that there are some things outside of your control, and sometimes you need to focus on your own bin and put the others aside for a while. If any of your issues belong in the second and third bins, you might need to let go of them and focus on your own bin.

It is also worth considering that two key causes of stress in life are financial and relationship stress. Relationship stress will be dealt with in Chapter 8, but let's consider financial stress here. For many people, financial concerns are a major cause of stress and anxiety, and often top the list of worries.

Many people live with severe financial stress. The triggers for financial stress will vary, but include bad debt, home loans, retirement, supporting the family and budgeting.[1] Financial stress often occurs when there are gambling issues, relationship breakdowns or job loss/unemployment. And the rising costs of utilities such as water or electricity can also add to the stress.

Financial stress can trigger health problems and substance-related issues and lead to being isolated socially. I recently spoke with a person who said that we have become focused on a 'Monopoly board' (we live in a material world), instead of on what we value in life such as family or meaningful activities. This seemed to be a very good description.

Advertising can be a driver to spend money we don't actually have. Writer and journalist Johann Hari talks about this in his book *Lost Connections*, explaining that since the 1920s, advertising has aimed to make us feel inadequate, and then offers the product as the solution to this. We are trained in our consumer society to feel a sense of scarcity or that there is 'never enough', and that purchasing lots of things will lead to happiness. The net result is acquiring more and more.[2]

The other aspect to our purchases is that they can trigger the release of dopamine in the brain (the same chemical messenger that is released when you gamble or take heroin). We can get a sense of happiness or a 'high' as a result, and so we may 'self-soothe' our moods with spending, and it can be addictive.

Awareness of these influences and the problems that can occur is the first step in dealing with troublesome financial issues. We will talk more about dealing with addictive behaviours, such as gambling or overspending, in Chapter 5. But one exercise to mention now is 'surfing an urge', as it can be very helpful when you are dealing with stress or anxiety, or any addictive urges.

HOW TO 'SURF AN URGE'

When you have an urge or craving (such as to gamble or overspend), it is helpful to remember that this urge is a bit like an ocean wave. A wave will build, peak, break at the shore and disappear. When surfing a wave, you stay on the board by keeping just ahead of the wave. Coping with an urge or anxiety is the same, as it will build and then go at some stage. To surf the urge or the anxiety:

- allow yourself to sit with it,
- focus on coping thoughts such as, 'it is anxiety and it will pass,' and
- use your breathing or relaxation techniques until it passes.

If you are concerned about your finances, it is important to have hope, work on the problem and maybe get some help. Financial counselling may assist. The peak body for financial counsellors in your country will be able to provide more information on these services or you can ask general counselling organizations where to get help. There are also apps to help reduce financial stress.

REDUCING FINANCIAL STRESS

- Talk about your financial concerns with someone you trust.
- Seek help from a financial counsellor.

- Problem-solve the issues (discussed in this chapter).
- Track your money by doing a budget or review your current budget.
- Work out what is causing financial stress (e.g. credit card debt, home loan).
- Reduce or get rid of your debt (e.g. gradually pay off credit cards, get rid of them or only have them for emergencies; talk about options related to your home loan with your lending organization).
- Avoid the 'pay afterwards' options now available.
- Set some goals and have a plan (e.g. paying off debt over a certain timeframe or increasing savings).
- Save up to ensure you have an emergency fund (e.g. put a regular amount away and let the amount grow!).
- Research purchases and do some comparisons.
- Separate what you 'need' from what you 'want' and let go of some of the wants.
- Delay when you shop — walk away and think about things for a while.
- Find ways to make more money to get yourself into a better financial place (e.g. doing some extra work from home).
- Research money-saving tips.
- Remember that small steps related to getting your finances in order add up to big steps!
- Maintain hope and a positive mindset (e.g. think about how good it will feel to get your debt down or to have more savings behind you).

Problem-solve some of the issues

Every day we face problems that need to be sorted. As a generalization, men seem to have a natural skill for coming up with solutions to fix things. But many still find dealing with problems stressful, especially when the number of problems is high.

We are going to look at how problem-solving life issues can effectively help reduce stress or anxiety. This is especially so when anxious feelings are overwhelming you. It helps you to think through a problem clearly, and to know where to start in dealing with it.

Problem-solving involves sorting out what the specific issues are, and looks at practical ways to deal with them. It helps you decide on the best possible solution for the problem (not necessarily the most perfect one). It is good to start with the simpler problems you face rather than the complex ones, to get your confidence up. Deal with problems one at a time and go through each step one at a time.

The steps involved in problem-solving are:

1. Define the problem in everyday and specific terms. This is important, so spend some time really thinking about this. An example of a problem might be: 'I am stuck in my job as a mechanic and I want to make a change, but I am worried about not having money.'
2. Make a list of all the possible solutions. Go wild with your brainstorming to generate as many solutions as you can (you can always discard the really wild ones)!
3. Think about the advantages and disadvantages of each solution.
4. Choose the best possible solution.

5. Think about any challenges that might be involved and how you will deal with them, then decide when you want to get the problem sorted.
6. Plan how to carry out the solution by breaking it down into steps.
7. Be realistic about whether you have the resources or time to carry it through.
8. Review your progress. Remember that even a partial success is a win, and you may not resolve the problem with the first possible solution.

This approach may seem straightforward to many men, but when anxiety is around, problem-solving can go out the window! It can be very effective, so have a go at working through one challenge that is causing you worry and see how you feel at the end of it.

SOLVING A PROBLEM (OR CHALLENGE)

Define the problem:

Make a list of all possible solutions:

Write out the pros and cons of each possible solution:

SOLVING A PROBLEM (OR CHALLENGE)

Choose the best solution (to start off with):

When will the problem be sorted out by? (Be realistic, and allow time to deal with potential challenges.):

Steps to carry out this solution:
1.
2.
3.

Review progress: Did the problem get sorted? Do you need to try a different solution?

Tap into talking therapies

Simply talking with someone who listens and is supportive can help you sort through feelings of stress or anxiety. As you talk, your brain is processing the events and your consequent thoughts and emotions. The key in this process is a trusting relationship with a therapist, and this is why finding a therapist you relate to is so important. Plus, there are particular therapies that have been shown to help with stress and anxiety. In this section we are going to focus on ideas and tools from cognitive behaviour therapy, acceptance and commitment therapy, mindfulness, and hypnotherapy. We will also provide some information about related issues, such as avoidance and performance anxiety.

When a lot of choice is presented to us, it can be overwhelming, and we can end up not choosing anything! So, take your time, read this section slowly, maybe a few pages at a time, and focus on trying out the tools as you go to decide which ones you are going to add to your toolkit.

Cognitive behaviour therapy

You might remember from Chapter 2 that cognitive behaviour therapy is based on the idea that our thoughts, feelings and behaviours (or actions) all influence each other. It is hard to change how you feel immediately (e.g. asking you to right now 'feel happy' will not work), but you can change how you feel over time by working with your actions or thoughts. Let's look at how this therapy can help reduce anxiety, starting with actions:

- Relaxation techniques come under actions and can help you feel calm.
- Doing activities that you enjoy and find relaxing (e.g. sport, road trips, seeing friends or playing music) can also help.
- Writing down your worries in a notebook or on your computer, and then putting the book or file away, can put the worries away too.
- Try allocating some 'worry time' each day (e.g. half an hour), during which you can worry, but not at any other time!

When you are anxious about certain things in life, you tend to avoid them. Examples include avoiding driving a car after an accident or after having a panic attack while driving, or avoiding going to an event or going on a plane, or perhaps using substances to zone out. Avoidance may relieve anxiety in the short term, but it can cause more distress in the long term. Here are a couple of stories illustrating avoidance:

> Ryan, a 45-year-old marketing manager, regularly attends meetings in other cities for his job. He gets very anxious with flying, and so he drives his car as much as possible, and if he flies, he drinks before and during the flight to cope.

> Peter, 38 years of age, had a panic attack while driving with his child in the car on a freeway. A truck moved into his lane, almost causing an accident. He will no longer drive on freeways or major roads, for fear of having an accident or another panic attack.

Exposure can help overcome avoidance. It is a tool that works on the idea that your brain might need to be rewired to not be fearful. Exposure involves facing the fear in a controlled way, that is, step by step. For example, if someone is fearful of spiders, exposure would involve looking at pictures of spiders, then going to a museum to look at dead specimens, perhaps looking at a small live spider in a jar at a distance, and then a larger one more closely.

TAKING CARE OF AVOIDANCE
Can you identify any activities you have been avoiding due to anxiety? Does your avoidance involve actions that might not be helpful? Jot down your thoughts below:

If you think avoidance is an issue, and that exposure might be helpful, consider getting some help from a therapist, or tap into information on exposure in books on cognitive behaviour therapy. (Refer to the Resources section at the end of the book.)

Now we'll look at 'thinking'. We have thousands of automatic thoughts a day, and probably half of them are not true! We have many potential errors or traps in our thinking. The following exercise gives some examples; read through them and see if any of them are familiar to you.

UNDERSTANDING THINKING TRAPS
1. Black-and-white thinking: There is no middle ground. Things are either black or white. For example, if one or two things don't work out for you, you think 'everything' is going wrong.

2. **Jumping to conclusions:** This is about making a negative interpretation of things. For example, you might interpret that someone is thinking negatively about you when there is no evidence of this (called 'mind-reading'). 'Crystal-balling' or jumping to negative conclusions about the future is another version of this.
3. **Catastrophizing:** This is overemphasizing the importance of events, so that a small mistake might be perceived as a disaster.
4. **Disqualifying the positives:** Discounting any positive experiences and maintaining a negative outlook.
5. **'Should' statements:** You motivate yourself via 'shoulds' and 'musts'. This is often related to setting high expectations for yourself, but the emotional results can be guilt or frustration.
6. **Labelling:** Applying labels to yourself, such as 'I'm a loser' or 'I'm a failure.'

With anxiety, pay attention to any 'what if' thoughts you might be having. Some of them are useful, such as: 'What if I don't pay my phone bill until next payday? No, if I wait that long my phone will get disconnected.' But most are usually not based on reality. They are future-based and we don't actually have a crystal ball in life.

Cognitive behaviour therapy teaches you to notice these thoughts and to challenge them. It involves a series of steps:

1. Notice how you feel and name the feeling (e.g. sad, worried, angry).
2. Notice your thoughts. What is your self-talk? ('I'm such a loser, I'm going to lose my job').
3. Ask yourself what the traps are in this thinking (e.g. catastrophizing the situation, crystal-balling or labelling).

4. Develop more helpful thoughts (e.g. 'Work is stressful right now as the company is making some cuts to staff. I can't control what they decide, so I'll keep working each day, and make some plans if I find I need to').

Now take one of your recent 'what if' thoughts and follow the same steps and see how it changes your feelings at the end!

HOW TO DEAL WITH 'WHAT IF' THOUGHTS
Write down the thought.

How do you feel?

Can you identify any thinking traps?

Try to come up with a more helpful thought.

How do you feel now?

Let's bring these ideas from cognitive behaviour therapy together with a couple of examples, firstly using it to manage panic episodes:

- Panic symptoms can occur in a 'cascade'. That means that often one symptom follows another (e.g. shortness of breath followed by palpitations followed by dizziness).

- Our thinking tends to get more panicky in a cascade (e.g. 'Oh no, it's back … it's getting worse … it might be my heart … what if I have a heart attack?').
- To interrupt the physical symptoms of anxiety you need to focus on breathing effectively.
- To interrupt the panicky thinking, have a mantra that you say to yourself (e.g. 'It's anxiety, I know what it is, just breathe and it will pass').

TIP: Make up a FIX-IT card for your wallet to help deal with panic. It might look like this:
Take a few slow breaths.
Self-talk: 'I know what it is — it's anxiety. It will be fine. Just breathe and it will pass.'

The second example is 'performance anxiety'. At the start of the chapter we mentioned that feeling some stress or anxiety can actually help you perform better, but when there is too much, our performance can be affected. This was identified in the 'Yerkes-Dodson Law', which basically states that an increase in arousal of the nervous system can boost performance, but once we go past the optimal level, performance starts to decline (see also the Resources section at the end of the book).

This idea can be shown with a graph. A footballer has to kick a goal in a match. If he remains on the left-hand side of the curve, he will do well, but if his arousal moves over into the right-hand side, he is likely to be feeling anxious and miss the goal.

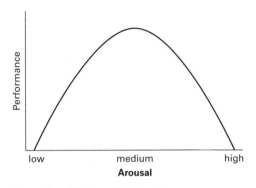

Example of Yerkes-Dodson Law

The same sort of changes in performance, whether at work or with a sexual partner, can occur when you have anxiety. It is often related to social anxiety or worry about what others will think. Using tools from the various therapies can help you stay on the left-hand side of the curve by:

- Remembering that it is normal to be nervous, that is, to put things in perspective.
- Being prepared for the event and familiar with the situation (e.g. the environment).
- Waiting for quiet if possible (e.g. before an event or talk).
- Using your breathing tools to reduce the symptoms of anxiety.
- Being mindful and staying in the moment rather than thinking about the outcome (e.g. as a musician, focus on listening to the music rather than judging your own performance).
- Being aware of your thoughts and challenging them or reframing them.
- Focusing on more helpful thoughts.

Athletes learn to 'label' their thoughts and feelings differently, and associate what they might have previously seen as negative as being a normal part of preparation. For example, if they notice their heart is racing, rather than viewing this negatively they focus on it as part of their preparation and then turn to breathing to manage it.[3] You will also see high-level athletes visualizing a good outcome before performing, such as at the start of a race or before doing a complex dive.

Acceptance and commitment therapy

Now let's look at the acceptance and commitment therapy (ACT) model, which is really useful for stress and anxiety. You might remember that there are six key processes involved in this approach, and we are going to look at them in more detail here in relation to managing anxiety:

1. ACT invites you to focus on your values or what is important to you, to live a more peaceful life. You can identify your values by considering what have been the most rewarding parts of your life so far, what has brought you joy, or what has inspired you or given your life meaning. You can also revisit the values exercise in Chapter 2.

2. Acceptance and commitment therapy incorporates mindfulness, which involves being in the moment on purpose. When you are mindful, you become more relaxed, you enjoy the moment, and are less likely to worry about the past or the future.

We have a 'being' or mindful part of the brain which pays attention to what is going on around us and a 'doing' or narrative part which involves a lot of thoughts and self-talk.

To function well, we need to be able to shift or move between these two states of mind. Here is an exercise to help you with this skill.

> ### LEARN TO SHIFT YOUR FOCUS
> - To learn to shift from our usual 'doing' mode in life to a more mindful 'being' mode, sit in a chair with your feet on the floor.
> - Have a look at your feet and connect with your thoughts about your feet! What thoughts come to mind? Maybe the places they have taken you, or problems they have caused you.
> - Now bring your attention to your feet without looking at them. Perhaps close your eyes and be aware of the sensations in your toes, the soles and upper part of each foot. Simply be aware of them and any sensations as you allow them to relax.[4]

Practise mindfulness as often as you can, such as when doing everyday activities like eating and drinking. Put aside some time to do this and turn off any screens and phones. Use your senses, so that when eating a strawberry, for example, notice what can you see, smell and taste as you slowly eat it. Or spend mindful time with children or a partner; even be mindful having a shower or doing household tasks. There are many mindfulness meditations which can help. Here is an example.

MINDFULNESS MEDITATION

Make yourself comfortable and allow your eyes to close. Take a little while to become aware of the sensations in your body and let yourself be still. Become aware of each part of the body and let go of any muscle tension, from the muscles in your face down through the shoulders and arms, chest and abdomen, legs, feet and toes. Allow relaxation to flow through your body, letting any tension ease away. Be aware if your mind wanders away from your focus on muscle relaxation. This is okay and happens from time to time. Be patient with yourself and gently refocus your attention on letting go.

For a while, too, be aware of your breath. As you gently breathe in and out, feel the air flow through your nose and lungs, then using your tummy breathing, breathe out, let go and relax.

Now practise mindfulness of sounds. Bring your attention to your ears and your hearing. Listen to the sounds around you. Simply be open to sounds as they arise and let them come into your awareness. Now release the awareness of sounds and be aware of any thoughts that come into your mind; observe them and sit with them for a while. You can be aware of thoughts and you can allow them to move on, just as you would observe clouds floating across the sky and then disappearing into the distance.

Then, when you are ready to be alert, simply become aware of the body again and slowly open your eyes, feeling comfortable and in the here and now. (You might like to check out mindfulness recordings and apps to assist.)

Notice the mention of thought awareness in the mindfulness meditation. This is really important. When practising mindfulness, your thoughts can easily stray, and the aim is to regularly bring your thoughts back to the here and now. Anxiety often leads thoughts into the future, and to worrying about things that might or might not occur. See where your thoughts reside at the moment with the next exercise.

3. Acceptance and commitment therapy talks about fusion and defusion. Fusion means being attached, and we can become 'fused' or very attached to our thoughts or feelings. Defusion is the opposite and means separating or stepping back from our thoughts, images and memories, and holding them gently rather than tightly. Defusion helps you realize that a thought is just a thought or information being generated in your brain, but not necessarily truth. Of our 60,000 thoughts a day, probably half need to go in the rubbish bin! Following is an exercise to help you understand defusion. If you can grasp this concept, it provides some of the most powerful tools in tackling anxiety.

UNDERSTANDING 'DEFUSION'
Imagine that your hands are your thoughts. Cover your eyes with your hands for a moment and imagine what it would be like to go around all day with your hands over your eyes. How would it limit you? What would you miss out on?

This is like fusion — we become so caught up in our thoughts that we lose contact with our here and now experiences, and we cannot function effectively. Imagine if you tried to drive, for example, while covering your eyes!

Now rest your hands on your lap — the act of moving your hands onto your lap is like defusion. You are more relaxed and are not going to be limited by any obstacle.

Now that you have a better understanding of defusion, here are some ways to put it into action.

TRY THESE WAYS TO DEFUSE YOUR THOUGHTS

- Notice a thought and say to yourself, 'I am having a thought that ...' or 'Thanks brain for the thought, but no thanks.' Or you can even say, 'F... off thought!'
- Imagine you are waiting at a bus stop, and a bus comes along but on the front of it is the wrong destination, so you choose not to get on it. Another bus then comes along with the correct destination and you decide to hop on. If instead of destinations, the buses displayed your thoughts, then you could choose which thoughts to go with and which ones to let pass by.

You also need ways to manage the feelings related to anxiety. The following defusion exercise is incredibly helpful, as it can allow you to sit with anxious feelings and defuse them.

SITTING WITH EMOTION

Think about a recent time when you experienced some anxiety (not the worst anxiety ever). Get in touch with the situation and the feeling of anxiety. Notice the feeling and where you feel it in the body. You might feel it in the chest or stomach or head. What shape or colour does it look like? Does it have a temperature or texture?

Create some space or light around the feeling and allow yourself to sit with it for a while. Notice your breath — the breath in and out. Imagine gently breathing into the feeling and keep breathing in and out to that spot in the body. Allow it to be there and breathe. Also notice what happens with the feeling. When you are ready, open your eyes and bring your attention back to the room.

4. Acceptance and commitment therapy highlights the role of 'acceptance' in tackling mental health issues, such as anxiety. Acceptance refers to making room for thoughts and feelings, even uncomfortable ones like anxiety, and reducing the struggle with them. It is often a challenge as we want to avoid feeling uncomfortable, but it is by staying with the discomfort that it can lessen.

WHAT ACCEPTANCE MEANS

Remember the old-fashioned movies where the bad guy falls into quicksand, and the more he struggles, the quicker he sinks? In quicksand, the worst thing to do is to struggle, but if you lie back, put your arms out and relax, you will remain afloat.

This is a bit like acceptance — it doesn't come naturally as your instinct is to struggle, but you can work on it and it helps. So, let go of the struggle as much as you can.[5]

5. This model also highlights two separate parts to the human mind: the 'thinking self' or thinking mind, and the 'observing self' or self-as-context. You may know the thinking mind well with its constant stream of thoughts, but the observing self may not be so familiar. The observing self is the part of the mind which notices your feelings and thoughts. Because of the observing self you can answer, 'What am I thinking' or 'How am I feeling?' It allows you to 'step back' and observe these things, but also remain separate from them. This part does not get hooked up in what the thinking mind is saying.

   You can use this part of the mind to help you with defusion. You might observe your thoughts and say, 'I am having a thought that ...' or 'Thanks brain for those thoughts.' This helps you recognize that they are just thoughts, no more and no less!

6. The final process is taking 'committed action' which means 'doing what it takes', even if this brings up some discomfort. It means recognizing that little change happens in life without action. Seeing a doctor or therapist, arriving at an appointment, reading self-help books, setting some goals or doing some regular meditation are examples of committed action.

TAKE ACTION — THE 'STRUGGLE SWITCH'

Imagine that at the back of your mind is a 'struggle switch'. When it is on, you are going to struggle against any emotional distress that comes your way. Anxiety may show up, and with the struggle switch on, you will do the best to get rid of it. But sometimes you end up being anxious about anxiety, or sad about it, or angry! The switch amplifies the problem.

But suppose that even when the struggle switch is on and anxiety shows up, you instead say, 'Okay, there's a knot in my stomach, my mind is telling me scary stories, it's unpleasant, but I'm not going to waste energy struggling with it. Instead, I am going to take action and do something meaningful.'

And what would happen if you turned the struggle switch off and anxiety showed up? What effect do you think this would have for you and the anxiety? (See the Resources section at the end of the book for more information.)

As you can see, acceptance and commitment therapy has a lot to offer in helping you to manage stress and anxiety. Well done for persisting and trying out the exercises. You might need to come back to them a few times to really take them on board. A final word on committed action!

TIP: Let this be your mantra: 'I don't have to feel like doing it, to do it!' Taking action is vital in tackling stress and anxiety (or when there are other mental health issues).

Hypnotherapy

Hypnosis is an altered state of consciousness (a trance), in which your mind is open to suggestions. It incorporates a range of relaxation techniques, and sessions generally include learning self-hypnosis, a practical tool that you can use to reduce anxiety.

A therapist can also give specific suggestions to help manage general worrying, anxiety about performance (e.g. giving a talk), social anxiety or panic episodes. They can also reinforce many of the tools covered during hypnosis. In addition, phobias (e.g. fear of flying or cats) can be treated through exposure in hypnosis.

TIP: Hypnotherapy can be very helpful in tackling stress and anxiety. You can learn self-hypnosis and practise it regularly. However, make sure to seek out a qualified hypnotherapist first. Hypnosis has been de-regulated in some countries, so look for therapists who are well-trained to treat anxiety using a range of approaches and have solid training in hypnotherapy. The websites of professional hypnotherapy organizations/associations can assist.

And wait, there is more that can help with anxiety! We are going to talk about a concept called 'self-compassion' in the next chapter, but it is important to mention it here, as men can be very self-critical about experiencing anxiety. Self-compassion means that you are understanding towards yourself when you are having a difficult time, rather than criticizing and judging yourself harshly. You can find out more about self-compassion in chapters 4 and 11.

Utilize self-help

Some men find it is useful to look at websites focusing on self-help or to read books like this one! (See the Resources section at the end of the book for more suggestions.) There are also helpful podcasts, apps and online programs. These often cover the sort of information already covered in this chapter or focus on a particular therapy.

Consider complementary therapies or medication

Some men find complementary therapies such as massage or acupuncture helpful. Some supplements like magnesium can also assist in anxiety.

When anxiety is severe and impacting your day-to-day functioning, it may be suggested you use specific medications in combination with talking therapies. Combining the two approaches can be more effective in severe anxiety than just using one, but medication should not be used without the talking therapies, as these create change for the long term.

It is best to discuss any potential role of medication with your doctor. The most common ones prescribed for anxiety are selective serotonin reuptake inhibitors (SSRIs) or serotonin-noradrenaline/norepinephrine reuptake inhibitors (SNRIs). If you use any of these medications, it is very important to follow the instructions carefully. Some general guidelines are:

- Start on a low dose to avoid side effects.
- Build up the dose slowly.
- Know that side effects often wear off after the first week or two.
- Medications take time to take effect (four to six weeks).
- Some can affect sexual functioning, so discuss the best option for you with your doctor.
- Do not stop taking the medication suddenly, but taper down the dose, and always do this in conjunction with your doctor, as they can help you monitor for any return of symptoms.

WHAT WE HAVE LOOKED AT SO FAR!

Stress and anxiety are part of life, but at times they can significantly impact your wellbeing. You now have a greater understanding about stress and anxiety and how your nervous system plays its part. Breathing techniques are a key tool in overcoming anxiety symptoms because of their calming effect on the nervous system.

It can be very helpful to talk to someone about stress or anxiety, and to learn a range of practical tools for managing these issues. Which tips or tools seemed to fit for you out of this chapter? One tool or approach may not suit everyone, so it is worth exploring a range to find out what works for you, and to then put them into practice regularly. And put them in your toolkit! Remember, the brain is constantly changing and practising your tools mindfully helps to rewire the brain and to build resilience. More on resilience later!

To finish up, here are some key tips from Alex about tackling stress and anxiety. As a musician, he is aware that many musicians struggle with performance anxiety at some point, and it is something that he has had to manage for himself. A recent tip that he has put into action is practising more mindfulness when performing music, rather than focusing on the outcome!

TACKLING STRESS AND ANXIETY

1. Learn as much as you can about stress and anxiety and remember that the physical symptoms won't cause you harm.
2. Focus on a healthy lifestyle — there are always things you can improve on.
3. Talk with someone you trust and let them know how you are feeling.
4. Get a medical check-up.
5. Reduce your 'stress bucket' wherever you can and learn to relax. Try breathing techniques or meditation.
6. Identify some of the things causing you stress and anxiety, and problem-solve some of them.
7. Look into the talking therapies — it can be good to share your thoughts and feelings and learn some tools to manage them.
8. Be kind to yourself and practise mindfulness each day.
9. Use some self-help resources, including apps.
10. Consider complementary therapies or medication if needed.

4.

OVERCOMING DEPRESSION

Every day begins with an act of courage and
hope: getting out of bed.
Mason Cooley

Life has good events and feelings, and life has suffering. Depression is a common life experience that involves suffering. It can occur at any age, and can be a major and potentially life-threatening problem, or it can be fairly short-lived and uncomplicated.

Depression feels awful, but there is always light at the end of the tunnel, so please hold onto hope. There are many approaches and strategies that can assist depression, and fortunately most instances pass in weeks or months.

This chapter is full of practical ideas and tools to deal with depression, so take your time reading through it. Practise the tools you see as best for you.

UNDERSTANDING DEPRESSION

There are many misconceptions about depression in the community. Having accurate information can allay fears and help men seek help earlier. So, let's start with some important information about depression.

You will hear various terms like 'clinical depression', 'organic depression' or 'major depressive disorder', but let's stick with the straightforward term of 'depression' in this book.

It is important to remember that sadness and depression are not the same. Sadness is often triggered by difficult life events, whereas depression may or may not be related to these. Feelings of sadness or brief depressive feelings are part of day-to-day life, but when a depressed mood persists for a period of time and is impacting your ability to function, it is a significant problem that needs to be addressed. In other words, depression is a more severe and persistent problem than sadness. Here are some key facts about depression:

- Depression is one of a number of issues we can have with mood.
- It is reported that 1 in 6 to 1 in 8 men will experience depression during their lives. This means that millions of men are affected by depression, and many are disabled by it and cannot function, such as not being able to work.
- Women are diagnosed with depression almost twice as often as men, but this doesn't mean that men have better overall mental health, that they are not suffering, or that the impact of depression is any less in men's lives. It may be that men are less frequently seeking help.
- Men with depression are known to report fewer symptoms than women, and men are less likely to seek help. As a result, and due to men not sharing how they feel as often, depression in men is often missed by health professionals.

- Suicide is a risk with depression. As stated earlier, male rates of suicide are very high around the world (we are going to focus more on this in Chapter 10).

The main features of depression are ongoing low mood and/or loss of pleasure or interest in activities that were previously enjoyed. Further signs of depression can be withdrawing from relationships, being very self-critical, being over-involved with work, being irritable or having angry outbursts. Other signs might be an inability to cry, turning to substances such as alcohol or illicit drugs to numb the feelings of depression, or other risky activities (e.g. driving fast, unsafe sex). To illustrate potential features of depression, consider Callum's story:

Callum, a 27-year-old barman, found himself for several months getting into a pattern of mostly going to work and then home again to sleep. He no longer went to the gym or visited his family. In fact, he took on as many shifts as he could to avoid seeing them. He was irritable with his work colleagues, and when he did go out socially, he would get drunk and use recreational drugs to escape.

You can see from Callum's story that the features of depression may not be readily apparent to him or his friends or family. Having knowledge about the symptoms is important and health professionals can assess for depression with tests.

If you are concerned about depression, you may choose to try the following 'screening test'. Screening tests give an indication that a problem may exist, but they do not diagnose the problem. If you find you respond positively to the questions below, you could seek some advice from a doctor or mental health professional to determine if depression is present.

A SHORT SCREEN FOR DEPRESSION

Over the past two weeks, have you felt sad, down and miserable in mood, or lost interest and pleasure in your usual activities? If you responded 'yes' to either of these questions, then depression may be present and you need to consider whether some of the other key features of depression are also problems for you, namely:

- weight gain or loss/increase or decrease in appetite
- sleep disturbance (e.g. difficulty getting to sleep or waking up early)
- feeling slowed down, or very restless/anxious
- feeling tired or having no energy
- lacking in sexual drive
- feeling worthless, excessively guilty, or hopeless
- having poor concentration or difficulties remembering things or making decisions
- having recurrent thoughts about death or suicide.

You can take an online depression self-test at: **www.blackdoginstitute.org.au/clinical-resources/depression/depression-self-test**. Note: Screening tests are available for people from various cultural backgrounds.

It is worth noting another potential problem with mood, namely bipolar disorder, in which there are strong changes in mood and energy. Sometimes bipolar disorder is identified late because it can be confused with depression early on. However, in bipolar disorder there are periods of:

- depression, and
- elevated mood or mania, often with agitation and overactivity, racing thoughts, little need for sleep and rapid speech.

The changes in mood can last a week or more, and affect your functioning, thoughts and behaviour. Bipolar disorder needs long-term management, which may include medication and psychological therapies. If you are concerned that you may have symptoms that fit with bipolar disorder, it is important to see a doctor.

OVERCOMING DEPRESSION

We are now going to look at various approaches that can help with depression. They take into account all aspects of you, and include reaching out for help, having a good assessment, improving your lifestyle, connecting with people more, seeing a therapist or considering medication. Let's look at all the approaches, as well as the tips and tools that may assist.

Reach out for assistance and learn more about depression

Swimmer Michael Phelps once said about depression:

> It was good for me to understand it's okay to not be okay. For me it was hard to put my hand out and ask for help. That's the one thing that probably singlehandedly changed my life and saved my life.[1]

Whatever the issues contributing to the depression, at times we all need to ask for some assistance. A good place to start is to talk to someone you trust, be it your partner, a family member, friend, work colleague or a doctor.

When men are asked by a doctor about how they are feeling

when they are being pushed around by depression, they often say something like, 'I feel terrible' or 'I feel like shit.' An understanding doctor will get what you are saying and ask more questions, so say it in any way that works for you, because the important thing is to let someone know that you are feeling down or struggling.

> ### KEY POINT
>
> Let someone know you are not okay or feeling down. It doesn't matter how you say it, just work on saying it.

What you don't understand fully can be frightening and overwhelming, and so it is helpful to know more about depression and its management. We know that taking some action early in dealing with depression is very important, and that the depression will generally improve over time and with treatment.

We also know that there are many myths about depression and its treatment and these can create stigma in the community. An example of a myth is that depression means 'weakness'. This is often expressed by men in the military, but it is also a myth generally in the community. In fact, many people will experience depression, and having depression means the person is facing challenges that take courage to overcome. Here are some important points about depression:

- Depression is not straightforward or due to the same things in everyone. It can arise from a whole range of factors.
- We don't fully understand what causes episodes of depression, but the risk factors for depression include:
    — a history of depression in the family

- — post childbirth, for men (about 10 per cent) as well as women
- — severe or chronic illness (for example, heart disease or cancer)
- — loss and grief due to relationship breakdown or loss of a partner due to death.
- Depression in men can be triggered by times of change or transition in life, such as relationship breakdown, loss of job/starting a job, divorce, having a baby, retirement. Loss and grief may be an element in change.
- Trauma from childhood, assaults or military service may also contribute to depression.
- We have a tendency to focus on negative thoughts as part of our survival, so they can become a trap at times, one negative thought generating more negative thoughts.
- It seems that when there is depression, certain chemical messengers in the brain (including serotonin) may be affected. The role of these messengers is not fully understood, and recent research suggests that inflammation may also play a role.
- When there is depression, there is greater risk of anxiety, substance use (often to self-treat the symptoms), or problems such as gambling. Anxiety itself can also trigger depression.
- Given that a number of factors can cause depression and that each man is unique, then management needs to address the factors relevant to that particular man.

Coming back to the fact that men are at risk post the birth of a child, men need to be included in the preparation for having a baby, around the time of the birth, and in care afterwards. Looking after your wellbeing, getting involved with classes and chatting to the midwives, or your doctor, are important. Good resources for new fathers are available. (See the Resources section at the end of the book.)

Have a thorough assessment and physical check-up, and look at your lifestyle

If you think that depression may be affecting you, then you need a thorough assessment. This involves sharing your story with a doctor and discussing the depression, your past medical history, family history, details of drug and alcohol use and social situation. A good assessment can help differentiate between depression and bipolar disorder, for example, and also identify other issues like anxiety or substance use.

As with anxiety, it's important to make sure that there are no underlying physical issues triggering low mood, such as low thyroid gland function, vitamin deficiencies or anaemia. A good health check-up is part of the assessment, and this will involve being examined and having blood tests.

It's also vital to have a good look at your lifestyle and see if anything is contributing to the depression, for example, not eating well, little exercise, lack of sunlight.

LIFESTYLE TIPS TO IMPROVE YOUR MOOD

- Appetite can be affected in depression. You may be eating less or more food or perhaps turning to unhealthy foods. Your brain needs good nutrition to function, so focus on eating healthy foods regularly (even if you are not hungry).
- Exercise is known to have a positive effect on mood. Perhaps start with some morning walks, as the morning light stimulates mood-lifting chemicals in the brain and aids sleep at night. Gradually build up the exercise with time.
- It is also good to schedule some pleasurable activities each day. Just plan each day at a time, and slot in some easy-to-achieve activities (e.g. going to the gym, seeing a friend, gardening or watching a movie). See the next section on talking therapies and 'planning some action'.
- Anxiety often occurs with depression, so taking some time out to relax is vital. This might be watching a film, listening to music or walking at the beach. And check out the various meditations described in Chapter 3.
- Getting out into nature has been shown to be helpful in depression and for improving sleep, whether that is time in the countryside or at the local park.
- It is also important to reduce your use of alcohol, cigarettes and other drugs when feeling depressed. They can worsen the depression or compound your problems.

- And don't forget to disconnect from your phone, tablet or laptop regularly. Our brain needs time away from being stimulated by technology, and it needs some silence too.

Trouble going to sleep, and waking up in the middle of the night or too early in the morning are often problems in depression. Strategies that can assist include:

- Going to sleep at a regular time each night and avoiding sleep during the day.
- Using regular ways to wind-down before sleep (such as a warm shower or listening to calming music).
- Dimming lighting during this time, which is important for letting the brain know it is time for sleep.
- Getting off screens at least an hour or two before bed (the longer the better and switch off blue light).
- Meditations for sleep, especially ones that incorporate muscle relaxation and visualizations.
- Exercising during the day so you are tired.
- Avoiding too much caffeine during the day/evening, and alcohol at night.
- Avoiding large, heavy meals in the evening.
- Eating food such as bananas or warm milk can calm you at night (because of the type of proteins in them).

Your doctor will also work out a management plan with you. This involves identifying the key issues (see the next section) of your depression, working on treatment goals with you and a plan of how to work towards the goals. This may involve support and education, lifestyle changes, or potentially seeing a therapist or taking medication. A good plan includes what to do in a crisis and strategies for preventing relapse in the future.

Identify and work on some of the issues contributing to the depression

We have said that many factors can play a part in depression. Sometimes it is easy to identify these issues, but sometimes it is not. You may recognize that certain 'external' issues related to family, work, relationships, finances, gender or sexuality have been playing a part. Perhaps there has been significant loss or grief in your life (death of a loved one, loss of health, job or marriage).

Remember the core human needs of safety, satisfaction and connection (see page 8). Depression may be triggered or worsened when these needs are not being met, such as basic housing and financial needs, some sense of contentment in life, or connection with others.

Humans need other humans, and we feel secure when we are connected to others. Isolation causes stress and contributes to a sense of loneliness or depression. It may seem that we are all connected to others via social media, but the connections can be very superficial and often cause comparison with others. We actually need connection with people to share things that matter or things we value.

Issues related to gender or gender identity and sexual orientation may be contributing to mood. There may be difficulty in acceptance or social stigma, body dissatisfaction or bullying.

There may also be internal factors playing a role. Certain personality traits can predispose someone to depression; for example, a tendency to be a perfectionist can lead to feeling extra pressure (more on this later). Also, some men hold an underlying belief that to be an 'okay person' they need 100 per cent approval from others, but of course, this is not possible.

Unfortunately, some people in your life may not actually be capable of giving approval. It may be that you crave approval from a parent, for example, but they struggle with this either because of their personality traits or because they never got it from their parents. Talking with a therapist about these sorts of issues can be helpful, with the ultimate aim of acceptance of the limitations in the relationship. To further explore this idea, let's go back to Callum, whom we met earlier in the chapter:

> Callum was diagnosed with depression. With his doctor, he identified that one of the main issues troubling him was his relationship with his father. Callum thought his father was disappointed in him because he had not completed his university studies and was working as a barman. Callum said, 'I never heard an encouraging word from my father, and no matter what [I] did, I could never get approval from him.' This became a key focus of therapy, with the aim of helping him develop acceptance of the relationship and to live his life according to his own values and goals.

Tap into talking therapies

As with stress and anxiety, talking with a therapist can be very helpful when feeling depressed. A number of therapies have been shown to be effective for men, such as cognitive behaviour therapy (CBT), acceptance and commitment therapy (ACT), and problem-solving. These therapies were introduced in Chapter 2.

A therapist will listen to your story and help you make sense of what is going on. They may suggest that you work on some short-term goals to begin with, such as doing some exercise (see 'Set some goals' on page 25). Sometimes the tiredness that comes with depression can be a barrier to this but, remember, this will fade over time. You can also get caught up with the idea that you need to *feel* like doing something to actually do it. You can still do an activity even if you don't feel very motivated to do it! The outcome of taking action is that you get a sense of satisfaction when it is done, and this can lift your mood! Here are some of the steps involved in taking action:

1. Do some planning, just one day at a time.
2. Start with easy-to-do activities.
3. Take very small steps (e.g. walking for 10 to 15 minutes).
4. Include some activities that give you pleasure.
5. Work towards getting back to a normal routine.
6. Keep a record to assist you (see the exercise below).

PLANNING ACTIVITIES

Date/time	Action/activity	Tick when done
Saturday 11 a.m. Sunday 4 p.m.	Walk the dog for 15 minutes Call a friend	

It can also be helpful to keep a mood diary to see what is actually going on (see opposite). Keeping the diary can lead to surprisingly big results, such as seeing that there are some better days and how often these are occurring, and that mood may be worse when tired or stressed, for example.

Keep the diary for at least a week and rate your mood each day. Use a scale from 0 to 10, where 0 refers to 'no depression' and 10 to the most 'severe depression'. And also notice any triggers to your mood and jot them down.

In depression, thinking can become more negative, and often self-blaming and self-critical thoughts occur (e.g. 'I'm such a loser!'). You may also have a negative view of the world and the future. Cognitive behaviour therapy can help you manage the negative thinking and low mood because it is based on the idea that the way we think and what we do influence how we feel (refer back to the model on page 38).

Cognitive behaviour therapy involves very practical tools, carried out in a series of steps:

1. Notice your thoughts (e.g. write them down in a mood diary).
2. Understand that some thinking is unhelpful and there are traps in your thinking. In depression common ones are 'black-and-white thinking', 'labelling' or 'catastrophizing' (see pages 74–75).
3. Identify any of the thinking traps.
4. Challenge the unhelpful thinking.
5. Come up with more helpful thoughts.

Read through the following information and do the exercises. These are designed to take you through the steps. To start with,

MOOD DIARY

Day	Monday	Tuesday	Wednesday	Thursday	Friday	Saturday	Sunday
Morning mood (0 to 10) Any triggers?							
Evening mood (0 to 10) Any triggers?							

here are some examples of common thinking traps that lead to unhelpful thinking. Examples of more helpful thoughts are also shown.

MANAGING THINKING TRAPS

Thinking trap	Unhelpful thought	More helpful thought
Black-and-white thinking (also called 'all or nothing')	I'll never be able to manage the new job.	I need to allow some time to learn my new job, and I know how to cope with some stress.
Labelling	I'm just 'hopeless'.	I'm having a tough time right now, but there are lots of things I have done well in the past.
Catastrophizing	What if I never meet anyone, I will always be alone.	There is time. Most likely I will meet a partner again.

Using the table on page 108, identify a few events from today, and some thoughts that you have had (either positive or negative) and with the more negative thoughts, have a go at each column. Remember that feelings are one word such as happy, sad or angry. When you identify a thought that is negative and maybe has some traps, then practise challenging it. To do this, ask yourself questions like:

- What is the evidence for and against the thought?
- Am I being too black and white? Am I catastrophizing or labelling?

- Is there another way to think about the situation?
- If a friend was saying this to me, what would I say to them?

These questions will help you come up with more helpful thoughts. Then see how you feel!

Mindfulness was introduced in Chapter 2. It can be difficult to practise mindfulness meditation when depression is severe, but it can be very helpful a bit later on. Mindfulness meditation has been shown to have positive effects on different parts of the brain, and it helps you to develop new ways of thinking and feeling.

Cognitive behaviour therapy and mindfulness have been combined into 'mindfulness-based cognitive therapy', which can be taught by individual therapists or in groups. It is based on the idea that as mood begins to lower, negative thinking patterns occur, and these trigger a vicious downward spiral, worsening the feeling of depression. This is what the spiral looks like. Can you relate to it?

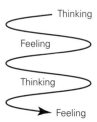

Rather than challenging thoughts, mindfulness-based cognitive therapy teaches you to be more aware or mindful of your thoughts and feelings, and to relate to them differently. The aim is to get less caught-up or hooked on them, and more tolerant of them.

WORKING WITH THOUGHTS

	What are you doing?	How do you feel?	What are you thinking?	Any thinking traps?	Use your challenges to come up with more helpful thoughts.	How do you feel now?
Sunday	At home watching TV.	Sad, worried.	I always stuff things up, I'm such a loser.	Black-and-white thinking, labelling.	I'm being too hard on myself; things will sort out.	Calmer and not as down.

To do this, see your thoughts and feelings as 'mental events' that you can witness. And remember that you are not your thoughts or feelings!

WATCHING THE WEATHER!

See your thinking as like the weather, which changes all the time, and comes and goes. Thoughts come and go like clouds in the sky. When you go hiking you might sit on a grassy hill and watch the clouds in the sky. In the same way, you can take a few moments to sit and notice your thoughts.

As a thought surfaces, ask yourself, 'Is it true?' So much of what we think about is untrue or based on assumptions. If the answer is 'no', then let the thought go. Perhaps imagine you put it on a cloud and watched it float away. [2]

There are many useful mindfulness tools to use in depression. Check this next one out!

TRANSFORMING NEGATIVE THINKING

Follow these steps to mindfully change negative thinking:
1. Recognize the thought (e.g. 'I'm not good enough, life is never going to improve').
2. Relax the body and release the thinking. Take a moment to breathe and relax.
3. Name a positive by thinking about 'what's actually good right now?' Maybe the answer is that you are safe and warm, or that you have a friend you can call.

In this way you get some distance from the negative thought, to relax and let go of it, and focus on more helpful thoughts. [3]

Depression can impact your ability to pay attention and concentrate. Here's an example of a mindfulness meditation that can help with this issue.

MINDFULNESS MEDITATION TO HELP WITH ATTENTION

1. Sit upright in a straight-backed chair, with your spine about an inch from the back of the chair, and your feet flat on the floor.
2. Close your eyes. Use your mind to watch your breath as it flows in and out. Observe your sensations without judgement. Do not try to alter your breathing.
3. After a while your mind will wander. Gently bring your attention back to your breath. The act of realizing that your mind has wandered, and bringing your attention back, is the key thing.
4. Your mind will eventually become calm.
5. Repeat every day for 20 to 30 minutes. [4]

Mindfulness-based cognitive therapy also encourages self-compassion. This means that you are more kind and understanding towards yourself when you are having a difficult time, rather than criticizing and judging yourself harshly. To practise self-compassion, remember that we all make mistakes, and try to put things into perspective rather than buying in to comparisons. Also, apply the 'golden rule' to yourself — treat yourself as you do others, with kindness and understanding! (You can find out more about self-compassion in Chapter 11.)

Ideas from acceptance and commitment therapy (ACT) can also be very useful when feeling depressed, as this approach teaches you to relate differently to your thoughts and feelings. This model suggests that, in depression, you become hooked on or 'fused' with thoughts about the past. This can cause unpleasant feelings, and you might then try to avoid these feelings. This can become a vicious circle and more negative thoughts can develop. Also, rumination or overthinking can occur. To reduce overthinking, you need to work on:

- Being less fused with or 'hooked' into your thoughts and feelings.
- Not avoiding uncomfortable feelings (see the 'Sitting with emotion' exercise on page 84).
- Ruminating less by focusing on the here and now, rather than the past or the future.

A simple tip to remember is that you have the power to choose which thoughts you pay attention to.

TIP: Choose your thoughts carefully. When you research a topic via Google, one search might come up with hundreds and hundreds of results. Don't pay attention to all of the sites identified but choose the ones that look most helpful to you. You can actually do the same with your thoughts, so give it a go!

An exercise that can assist in managing depression is the 'tug-of-war with a monster metaphor'. It is based on the idea that we can struggle with depression, and sometimes we need to reduce our sense of struggle to feel better.

TUG-OF-WAR WITH A MONSTER

Imagine that you are in a tug-of-war with a depression monster. You have one end of the rope and the monster has the other, and there is a pit in the middle. What do you need to do to prevent falling into the pit? The answer is not to pull harder, but to drop the rope or the struggle.[5]

If you want to explore some of these ideas more, have a look at books by author Dr Russ Harris. Also, the series of books by Mark Manson particularly appeal to young men. His book, *The Subtle Art of Not Giving a F*ck*, focuses on learning to accept your limitations and that it's okay not to feel great all the time. Negative experiences are part of life and understanding this will help us struggle less with unhelpful thoughts and feelings.

TIP: Check out the YouTube clips explaining some of the ideas behind acceptance and commitment therapy. 'Passengers on the Bus' illustrates how we are the driver in our lives, and often have disruptive and noisy passengers (thoughts) on board. The way to effectively deal with them is to accept and acknowledge them, and to drive in a direction that you think fits with your values.

Before we go on and look at a few more approaches, take a moment to reflect on what tips and tools you might take from the therapies described above to practise or to put in your toolkit for later!

Reflect on which tools from the therapies discussed so far might assist you. Jot down a list to refer to later on.

Ideas from positive therapy can also help you tackle depression. Positive therapy is not about feeling happy all the time, because we naturally experience a range of emotions, but it provides many useful ideas to improve your mental health.

As mentioned earlier, our minds have a tendency to focus on negative thoughts, as this is part of survival. The man who says there is no danger in a crocodile-infested river and then swims across it is less likely to survive than the man who says, 'There might be crocodiles, so I think I'll take the bridge.' This is why we have to work hard at fostering positive thoughts, not only to survive, but to feel good.

We actually need a ratio of three positive thoughts to one negative thought to feel good (to have a better mood and be relaxed). When depression is around, there are more negative thoughts and often more anxiety, and so you need to work on the ratio. You can do this by planning or creating more positive experiences into your days (e.g. seeing a friend, going for a walk), and tapping into happy memories or watching a comedy can also shift your thinking.

Make use of the positivity ratio. To tip your mood into a positive one, we need a ratio of three positive thoughts to one negative thought. Keep working at it each day by being aware of your thinking, using the tools you have learnt and planning more positive experiences.

Another way to encourage more positive thoughts and feelings is by practising gratitude. Even when life is very stressful, it is still possible to be grateful for things in your life (e.g. a good friend or the ocean), and this can help you cope. In fact, if you are feeling stressed or anxious, stop and focus on what you are grateful for and the anxious feelings will subside.

Research suggests that to improve mood, we need to write down or say out loud three things that we are grateful for once a week. You could say them while you are in the shower or out walking!

Remember Wayne from Chapter 2? He and his wife would have a cup of tea each Sunday afternoon, and say out loud to each other what they were grateful for from the week. They enjoyed this time together and Wayne found it helped his wellbeing.

It is worth tapping into gratitude regularly to notice the effect it has on your mind.

There is another approach called 'narrative therapy' that can help with depression. In a nutshell:

- Men create sense and meaning in their lives with stories, which are made up of events. We have stories about our abilities, challenges, dreams, failures, work and relationships.
- Some stories are more dominant than others and full of problems (e.g. 'I am a failure' or 'I am not good enough.'). We tend to fit events that happen in life into these dominant stories.
- Society influences our taken-for-granted beliefs in life and these stories, such as the story about the ideal male being strong and muscular and not emotional.
- We forget that there are always *alternative* stories, such as being competent at various things in life or having a range of strengths.
- In addition, the person and problem tend to be seen as one and the same. For example, a man with depression may view themselves primarily as being depressed,

somehow weak and to blame, rather than a competent individual who is being affected by depression. This can result in feeling helpless to take action. But remember that you are travelling through life and change is always possible!

Narrative therapy invites you to consider a number of questions about depression. Have a look at them and consider your answers.

NARRATIVE QUESTIONS ABOUT DEPRESSION

- What are some of the views held within our society about people who experience depression?
- How has depression impacted your view of yourself?
- Think of a time when in some small way you have been able to stand up to depression and have stopped it pushing you around.
- What qualities, skills or abilities did it take for you to resist depression in this way?
- How can you use these qualities, skills, abilities or strategies in the future to continue to challenge depression?
- Depression can dominate our lives and make it hard for us to see how we have resisted its tricks and traps. Think back through your life to other times when you were able to outsmart depression and describe what happened.
- If you were to continue to challenge depression in this way, how would your life be different?
- Think of someone who is special to you and knows you well. What would they predict for your life if they were made aware of your success over depression?
- What kind of person are you in the process of becoming, and what would your special person/s say about this?
- How are you going to celebrate your achievements?

These questions help you to relate to depression in a different way. It has pushed you around and you are much more than depression. In addition, remember that you have many strengths and tools to overcome it.

Work on perfectionism

Do you tend to be a perfectionist and want to do things extremely well? Or do you expect perfection in others? Sometimes we inherit a tendency to be a perfectionist, and often we learn it. Perfectionism may appear in different areas of life, including your appearance, weight, fitness, how you perform at work or socially, cleanliness, music or sport. And rates of perfectionism seem to be increasing worldwide.

Perfectionism can be viewed as a 'friend', helping you to do a good job and be productive, or it can be regarded as a 'foe', as it is really an illusion (perfection is not actually possible). It can be involved in disappointment and depression in life, because it results in putting pressure on yourself to meet really high standards.

The underlying beliefs that can be involved in perfectionism include needing approval from others, to be 100 per cent competent in life, and needing to feel in control. These beliefs lead to traps in our thinking, especially 'black-and-white thinking', for example, 'If I don't do really well with this task, then it is not worth doing' or 'I must do things perfectly and never fail!' These patterns also lead to self-critical thinking and defining your self-worth by how well you perform.

Perfectionism can lead to monitoring (checking appearance or cleanliness excessively), avoidance (e.g. not making decisions, avoiding social situations), procrastination, hoarding or seeking reassurance. It can be a factor in anxiety or depression. It is a common trigger to peri- or postnatal issues (around or after the birth of a child), with a sense of wanting to be the perfect parent and finding that this is really hard to measure up to as babies do things in their own way and time!

KEY POINT

There is a big difference between healthily striving to do a good job, and unhelpful striving for perfection.

Here is the story of Johnny who was feeling depressed. It became apparent as he told his story that he was a perfectionist:

> Johnny is a 33-year-old IT consultant. He excelled at university and has worked hard in his roles ever since. He is known to be very conscientious, but his manager has noticed that he has been falling behind in his tasks.
>
> Johnny has not been sleeping well, feels tired a lot of the time, and has stopped playing tennis. He always worries about making mistakes and doing an excellent job. Since the manager picked up some errors in his work, Johnny has been taking extra time on tasks, but is finding he can't concentrate and is tending to put them off.

We will come back to Johnny in a short while, but to see if perfectionism is an issue for you, look at these statements and note if they are true or false:
- Nothing good comes from making mistakes.
- I must do things right the first time.

- I must do everything well, not just the things I know I'm good at.
- If I can't do something perfectly then there is no point even trying.
- I rarely give myself credit when I do well because there's always something more I could do.
- Sometimes I am so concerned about getting one task done perfectly that I don't have time to complete the rest of my work.[6]

If you have answered 'true' (even if somewhat true) to most of the questions, then perfectionism might be something you want to work on.

Part of being a professional musician is being a perfectionist and aiming to give a great performance. Following are some tips that Alex has researched and worked on for managing perfectionism.

DEALING WITH PERFECTIONISM

- Be aware of your own and others' expectations and ask yourself if they are realistic.
- Remember that doing things perfectly does not necessarily make others see a person as more worthy.
- Sit back and reflect, rather than rushing in and working your usual way.
- Weigh up the advantages and disadvantages of being a perfectionist. You may want to let go of some of the disadvantages.
- Experiment with doing a 'good enough' job instead of a perfect job and see how it goes.

- Stop comparing yourself with others (this is a BIG one in today's world).
- Think about whether you need to put some time limits on different tasks, and work to the set time rather than doing the job perfectly.
- Be aware of any fears that are hiding behind perfectionism (e.g. fear of failure or of criticism), then deal with the fears.
- Be aware of your thoughts and challenge 'black-and-white' thinking (see page 74). Make efforts to keep things in perspective.
- Practise relaxation and mindfulness (e.g. a musician focusing on the music being played rather than thoughts about doing a perfect job).
- Be kind to yourself in your thinking and actions.
- Aim for more flexibility and recognize that change is always possible.
- Remember, very few things are perfect. Sometimes we need to aim for a 'middle path' in what we do, rather than an extreme. Dare to be average some of the time!

You might find it helpful to make use of some questions to challenge thinking around being perfect. Examples might be:
- Who says that I must always be perfect?
- What would happen if I made a mistake occasionally?
- Would it be the end of the world if I made a mistake?
- What is the worst thing that could happen?
- Would making a mistake be so terrible? Could I live with that?

And sometimes doing an experiment with behaviours can be useful when perfectionism is around. For example, if you like to always respond to text messages within a few minutes, experiment with not responding so quickly. You might predict that some people may notice you are not responding in the same way, so be prepared for that, but see what happens! It is likely that you will both adjust!

Tied in with perfectionism is procrastination or putting things off (more avoidance!). Procrastination might be used to avoid a stressful situation, such as delaying a work project. Sometimes using distractions, like the internet, watching movies or smoking, is a form of procrastination.

Procrastination can be related to high expectations (e.g. wanting the work to be perfect), or it may also stem from a fear of failure or criticism, a fear of uncertainty, a desire to be approved of by certain people in your life or a desire to be in control of things. Sometimes it is related to self-doubt. Let's come back to Johnny:

Johnny saw a therapist through an employment assistance program. He heard Johnny's story and talked to him about perfectionism and procrastination. They talked about the background to it and used cognitive behaviour therapy to tackle some unhelpful thinking and core beliefs. Johnny's mood gradually improved and he returned to tennis. He also joined a meditation class and was surprised that he enjoyed it!

And to finish this section, here are some suggestions for overcoming procrastination:

- Be aware of what is driving it (e.g. fear of failure).

- Challenge your thoughts and underlying beliefs (e.g. high expectations) and develop new perspectives on yourself.
- Replace the word 'should' with 'choose' in your thoughts.[7]
- In terms of wanting to be in control or fear of uncertainty, challenge some of the ideas about control as life does involve uncertainty.
- If you are using distraction to avoid a task, weigh up whether the distraction comes at a cost. It is also important to be honest with yourself and ask whether or not the avoidance is needed.
- Set more realistic goals for yourself. Breaking them down into small steps can help (see page 26).
- Plan your day as we all have times of more energy or motivation (e.g. first thing in the morning or at night), and plan to do important tasks at those times.
- Learn to sit with unpleasant feelings, rather than distracting yourself from them (see the 'Sitting with emotion' exercise on page 84).

Cognitive behaviour therapy is very helpful in managing perfectionism and procrastination. Refer to the earlier descriptions of this therapy in the book and to the Resources section at the end.

Manage change and transition in life

Bill's story below highlights the impact that change and transition can have on mood, particularly when a number of changes occur over a short period of time.

Bill is a 39-year-old man who works as a manager at an advertising firm. In recent months he has been worrying a lot and feeling low in his mood. In the past two years, there have been some major changes in his life — a job change, moving house and the birth of his third child nine months ago.

Bill is also having difficulty sleeping, and he is drinking a bottle of wine each night to try to get to sleep. He is not able to focus at work, and his boss is starting to ask questions. Bill's partner has noticed that he no longer goes to the gym, and that he seems to be more withdrawn from her and the family.

Bill had found these life transitions challenging, especially changing jobs and being stressed about the new role in the first month. Then soon after becoming a father again, he found managing the demands of several children difficult, including a restless baby.

Depression is often related to a period of change or transition in roles (such as starting a new job or losing a job), migration, having a baby, or retiring. Change in life can be very stressful as it can be hard to deal with uncertainty in life — we like to have a sense of control and security. Change can also trigger a whole lot of different emotions, including fear, and a sense of loss and grief (we will look at loss and grief in detail in Chapter 6).

Times of change or transition in relationships can also occur at different times in life and may be important factors in depression. For young men, a break-up can be very difficult to cope with, and for older men divorce may be a key factor. Transitioning to becoming a father can be challenging, and there may also be illness-related transitions, such as developing a chronic illness like arthritis or heart disease or being diagnosed with cancer.

With the loss of a relationship, there is a series of phases including before the separation, during the separation (when there can be confusion and disbelief) and finding a new identity and adapting after the separation. It is a process that takes time, and we can move backwards and forwards in this process.

Ageing can be seen as a transition. Men may find the mid-life phase (40 to 65 years of age) challenging. There may be new job responsibilities, or changes in relationships. Self-doubt can occur if life goals have not been reached, even a sense of 'failure'. There may be boredom or confusion to cope with. Irritability, anger or depression can occur.

In terms of retirement, changing ideas about identity can be a challenge. While working, identity might have centred around being a provider, being useful or achieving. To adjust, you need to realign your sense of self and what you are basing your self-worth on now. The focus in retirement may be less about doing and more about being yourself. You may move towards being involved in the community or being there for your partner or grandchildren. Here are some strategies for dealing with periods of change or transition:

- Draw out a timeline of when the changes occurred and think about whether the depression symptoms arose around these times.
- Explore the range of feelings that are being experienced, including sadness, anger or grief. Sometimes it is hard to express these, so try writing or talking about them. You might want to seek out a therapist.
- Work on accepting that an old phase in life or a role has been lost (e.g. loss of a job, children leaving home).
- See your new role(s) in life more positively by thinking about any benefits or possibilities coming from them. List them out!

- If your self-worth has been challenged by the changes, then work on this (see page 285).
- Look after your health and wellbeing (e.g. get regular exercise and sleep, and eat healthy foods).
- Tap into some of the tools for managing stress outlined in Chapter 3.
- Foster a positive frame of mind.
- Remember to make use of your strengths as you adapt and remain true to your values.

Engage in meaningful activity and social connection

We have looked at activity being central in our lives (see pages 40–41), but sometimes in depression there can be a loss of motivation or energy, which means that you may find it harder to do the activities that you usually engage in or enjoy. This can cause a vicious circle of doing less and feeling worse.

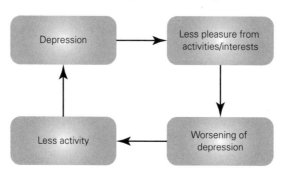

There are various ways you can start to engage in activity. Remember, you don't need to feel like it to do it, but sometimes you will feel better after doing the activity. As Manson reminds us, 'Don't just sit there, do something!'[8] Consider realistic goals for yourself (see page 26) and start small! Do some planning and begin with small steps (e.g. having a shower, going to the letterbox, eating a healthy meal) and build up. As you become more active, focus on the activities that you find pleasurable or give you a sense of satisfaction. Ask yourself what do you usually enjoy or find meaningful? (Also see the tips on taking action on page 103 and the strategies for working on motivation on page 142.)

When men feel depressed or have lost a job or separated from a partner, they can feel very isolated. Loneliness can be a significant issue and can be tied in with a feeling of abandonment. We all need other humans, or a sense of connection with other people, so dealing with this is very important to your recovery. Following are some tips on dealing with loneliness.

DEALING WITH LONELINESS
- Remember loneliness is a feeling, not necessarily a fact.
- Loneliness can trigger negative thinking, so watch out for this and challenge it.
- Take action and phone or visit family members.
- Reconnect (phone, email, meet up) with friends or past friends or work colleagues.
- Head out to places with people, such as the beach or shopping centres and have some contact by saying hello and having a chat with shop assistants.
- Find an education group about depression and link with others via the group.
- Take up a hobby or take a class or join a group.

- Focus on the needs or others (e.g. volunteer your time or services).
- Listen to the radio, including talk-back radio. Think about phoning in!
- Call a support service or line.

....

Use self-help

Many men find it helpful to read about treatments of depression or to do some online treatment programs. Given you are the expert on yourself, or maybe you prefer to work through things at your own pace or privately, there are some great resources available including books, online resources and courses, and apps. See the Resources section at the end of the book for more information. Here's how Bill, from earlier, took action:

Bill went to see his doctor and had a check-up. The doctor commented that a lot of change had happened in Bill's life over recent months, and no doubt this had triggered some worry. He also said that a depressed mood can follow a period of anxiety.

The doctor talked with Bill about reducing his alcohol intake at night, and about ways to help him sleep. Getting some exercise was an important tool to help with sleep and mood, and Bill was keen to get back into jogging and playing squash with a friend.

After talking about treatment options, Bill decided he would not see a therapist initially, but that he would do an online program which used cognitive behaviour therapy. The doctor organized to see him again and monitor his progress, and they talked about Bill seeing a therapist down the track, if need be.

Consider complementary therapies or the role of medication

You may want to look at complementary therapies to assist in managing depression. Examples include:

- Massage.
- Various herbal medicines or supplements are used for mild depression, such as St John's Wort. Remember that complementary medicines can have side effects and interactions with other medicines, so always discuss complementary medicines with a health practitioner, and always let your doctor know what you are taking.
- Fish oils (omega-3 supplements) as there is evidence they have a beneficial effect on mood. (These are not to be used in bipolar disorder or if taking blood thinner medications.)
- Vitamins B9 (folate) and B12, as research on their benefits is promising.
- Light therapy for seasonal depression (when depression is worse in the winter months due to less sunlight). There are special light glasses that help with seasonal depression.

When depression is really pushing you around and your symptoms and their impact are severe, it is suggested you use medications alongside talking therapies. Combining the two approaches can be more effective in moderate or severe depression, than one alone. As was said for anxiety, medication should not be used in depression without the talking therapies, as these create change for the long term.

It is important to discuss any potential role of medications with your doctor. The most common ones prescribed for depression are selective serotonin reuptake inhibitors (SSRIs) and serotonin-noradrenaline/norepinephrine reuptake inhibitors (SNRIs). If you use any of these medications, it is very important to follow the instructions carefully. Some general guidelines are to:

- start on a low dose to avoid side effects
- watch for common side effects such as nausea and headaches
- know that side effects often wear off after the first week or two
- build up the dose slowly
- know that antidepressant medications take time to take effect (four to six weeks)
- know that some can affect sexual functioning, so discuss with your doctor
- not stop them suddenly but taper the dose down slowly, and always do this in conjunction with your doctor, as they can help you monitor for any return of symptoms.

It is vital to see you doctor regularly after starting medication to check on progress as well if any side effects are occurring. Rarely will someone feel more depressed with worsening suicidal thoughts in the weeks after starting medication, but if this is happening, your doctor needs to know this and take appropriate action.

Medication is generally used for a minimum of six to twelve months when you have depression for the first time. Don't panic at this point! What you need to remember is that the medication is helping you feel and function better, but the underlying depression has to resolve and heal. When more than one episode of depression has occurred in life, you may need medication for several years, and some find they are better being on it long term.

Develop a relapse prevention plan

Depression can sometimes relapse or return. Many people will recover from depression and not experience another episode, but some will have a second episode and a smaller number will have a more chronic course. This is why it is important to have a relapse prevention plan in place to give you some reminders if symptoms re-occur. There are three steps in developing a plan for managing depression relapse:

1. Identify the early warning symptoms, such as difficulty sleeping, ruminating, withdrawing from friends.
2. Identify possible high-risk situations for relapse, such as stress or being overtired. Consider strategies to protect yourself, for example, taking some time out or using relaxation exercises.
3. Prepare an emergency plan to put into action when the depression is relapsing, such as keeping an eye on your thinking, getting support from friends or family, making an earlier (or urgent) appointment with your doctor and using medication if that was helpful last time.

Filling in a relapse prevention plan template can be useful, so you can have it at the ready.

RELAPSE PREVENTION PLAN

My early warning signs
1.
2.
3.
4.

Possible high-risk situations for me
1.
2.
3.
How to cope with high-risk situations:

My emergency plan for relapse

One of the key causes of depression relapse is continued negative or pessimistic thinking, so doing the talking therapies, and mindfulness in particular, is vital. There is more information on prevention in Chapter 11 and we talk about suicide prevention in Chapter 10.

WHAT WE HAVE LOOKED AT SO FAR!

The subject of depression is very broad. Depression can be a common and serious problem and talking with someone early is important. There are many triggers to depression in life and identifying these and working on them can help. Support from an understanding doctor and talking therapies can assist.

Another good thing to remember is that you are not the depression. If you can view it as external to yourself, then you can see how it is pushing you around. And you can use all of your internal and external resources and tools to manage it.

Working on your thinking is vital, as negative thinking worsens in depression and can hook you in. This does take effort and work, but is well worth it, both to recover from depression and to prevent relapse. Use the tables in this chapter to record your thoughts and challenge them.

Work with mindfulness, and with the various ideas from acceptance and commitment therapy (ACT), especially defusing negative and uncomfortable thoughts and feelings. Remember too that even if you don't feel like it, engaging with other people and activity is vital. The benefits are large. Always know that help is available and that there are many tools that can help you feel better. Let's finish with some tips for managing depression.

TIPS FOR MANAGING DEPRESSION

1. Reach out for assistance and learn more about depression.
2. Have a thorough assessment and physical check-up and look at your lifestyle.
3. Identify and work on some of the issues contributing to the depression.
4. Tap into talking therapies.
5. Work on perfectionism.
6. Manage change and transition in life.
7. Engage in meaningful activity and social connection.
8. Use self-help resources, including apps.
9. Consider the role of complementary therapies or medication.
10. Develop a plan to prevent relapse.

5.

MANAGING SUBSTANCE-RELATED ISSUES AND ADDICTIONS

The bravest sight in the world is to see a great man struggling against adversity.
Lucius Annaeus Seneca

This chapter looks at substance-related issues and a number of addictions that men may experience, including gambling and addictions to pornography and technology. For all of these issues, there are common themes in terms of causes and treatment.

An addiction is defined as a strong and compulsive need (i.e. a powerful impulse) to regularly have something (e.g. a drug) or to do something (e.g. to gamble), despite it causing you harm. It results in the inability to stop using the drug or doing the behaviour. With substances, the word 'dependence' is often used rather than addiction, referring to a physical reliance or craving for the substance, resulting in issues such as withdrawal.

Many people see addiction as 'natural', as we all experience moments of addiction in life, like with romance. The brain responds to a range of experiences (e.g. eating favourite foods, having sex, getting high on drugs, winning a bet) with pleasure. Various chemical messengers in the brain, including dopamine, are released, which causes us to feel high. This acts as a reward and we often repeat the behaviour as a result.

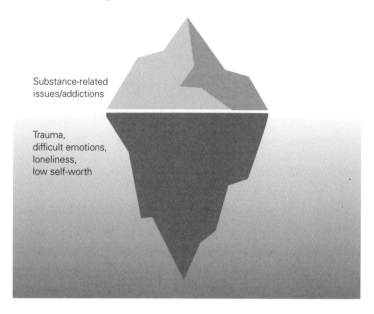

Substance-related
issues/addictions

Trauma,
difficult emotions,
loneliness,
low self-worth

Substance-related issues and addictions can also be seen as the tip of an iceberg. The substance-related issues sit above the water, and what lies under the water might include factors such as trauma, difficulties coping with feelings, lack of connection with others or struggles with learning or self-worth. These factors need to be identified, understood and worked with to help overcome the issues.

Let's hear more about Tim's story (some of it was shared in Chapter 2):

*Tim was struggling with gambling and substance use. It had
escalated over the past year, and he was feeling lost. He had
started using substances to cope with anxiety. He initially found
a couple of beers helped, but as time went on, the amount of
alcohol he was consuming increased, and recreational drugs
became a regular part of his life. And he found over time that he
couldn't stop gambling or using substances, and that they were
creating new worries and problems.*

*Tim and his family were very concerned as he had lost a
good job, his girlfriend had 'given up' on him, his finances were
a mess and his self-confidence was at an all-time low. He had
always had trouble managing his temper, and this seemed to be
way more difficult now.*

SUBSTANCE-RELATED ISSUES

Unfortunately, men experiencing substance-related issues may
not recognize that there is a problem, or they may not be willing
or able to reach out for help. Also, when seeing a doctor or health
professional about other health concerns, men may not be asked
about their substance use, so any issues may not be picked up.

Substance-related issues are very common in our communities,
and a range of substances are used:

- A survey carried out in Australia in 2016 found that just
  under 4 in 10 Australians either smoked daily, drank
  alcohol in ways that put them at risk of harm, or used
  an illicit drug in the previous twelve months. [1]
- In 2019, the prevalence of illicit drug use (in the past
  year) in the United Kingdom was 1 in 10 adults. [2]
- In the USA, it is reported that there are over 22 million
  people who have a substance-related problem. [3]

- Approximately 50,000 New Zealanders receive support to reduce their alcohol or drug use every year, and this is thought to represent only one-third of those who are experiencing problems with use. [4]

About substance use

A substance (e.g. alcohol, drugs) refers to anything that is used to produce a 'high' or to alter the senses, our perception or how conscious or alert we are.[5] Humans use various drugs for medical reasons and for recreation.

Substances used for recreation include alcohol, cannabis, hallucinogens, inhalants, opioids, sedatives and drugs that reduce anxiety, stimulants (e.g. amphetamine-type substances, cocaine), tobacco and other substances. Many substances create an effect similar to the pleasure response in the brain, releasing chemicals such as dopamine or endorphins (pain-relieving chemicals). Here are some facts about men and substance use:

- In general, rates of substance use increase with age during the teenage years, and peak in early adulthood. Men aged 45 to 64 years of age have high rates of chronic excessive alcohol use.
- Alcohol and tobacco are responsible for 90 per cent of deaths related to substance use, and the riskiest substances include heroin, cocaine, tobacco and alcohol.[6] The current patterns in western countries are that younger people are smoking and drinking less and later.
- The way men use substances (e.g. bingeing, occasional or continual use) and their reasons for using them will vary (e.g. as an 'experiment', to 'escape', to 'join in' with

mates, the feelings it gives them, or to get through a certain situation).

- Men have higher rates of substance use and dependence than women, particularly with alcohol. Men are more likely to have alcohol-related accidents, as well as problems at work and issues with violence. Issues with substance use in men can be made worse due to taking risks or acting impulsively.
- If men are dependent, then the substance use takes on a life of its own and starts to take over the person's day-to-day experience. Some men develop mental and behavioural disorders due to substance use and addictive behaviours.

Withdrawal can occur when some drugs are stopped after using them for a long time, causing symptoms such as anxiety, hallucinations or insomnia. Some of these symptoms can be life-threatening (e.g. seizures).

There are harmful patterns of alcohol use, causing damage to one's physical or mental health, or behaviours leading to the mistreatment of others. And disorders relating to depending on alcohol may include cravings to use alcohol and increasing tolerance to it (needing more of the drug to get the same effect).[7]

Underlying trauma, anxiety or depression, schizophrenia or sleep problems, can be associated with using substances. Men may try to self-medicate with alcohol, for example, to ease their symptoms.

Some physical health problems, such as heart disease, lung disease and chronic pain can trigger substance use. Unfortunately, the substances can make the symptoms worse, and add new problems, such as drink-driving offences or arrests.

Many causes or risk factors for the development of substance-related issues have been suggested and include:

- Genetics (e.g. issues with alcohol may be present in parents or grandparents).
- Early environmental issues, such as childhood neglect or abuse.
- Using substances early in life.
- Social or cultural issues:
    — having parents or friends who use substances
    — social acceptance of substance use (e.g. in Australia using alcohol to relax and socialize is very much part of the culture, and in some cultures, intoxication is more accepted in men, and binge drinking may be viewed as 'masculine')
    — poverty.
- Having had childhood attention deficit and hyperactivity disorder (ADHD) or 'conduct disorder' (repeatedly violating the rights of others with aggression or deceit).
- Stresses such as:
    — having difficulty expressing feelings and using substances to cope
    — identifying as gay, trans-sexual or with another gender or sexual identity[8]
    — experiencing loss and grief.
- Difficulties coping with various life challenges:
    — not managing at school or at work, or not having activities to do in the community
    — low self-confidence
    — lack of supports
    — lack of coping skills (e.g. coping with anger, conflict).

Research has shown a number of negative effects of substance use.

- Excessive alcohol increases the risk of physical injury from accidents and violence. Young men are at risk of memory loss and unwanted sexual activity (being assaulted, assaulting others).
- Long-term risks from alcohol use include liver and heart disease, cancers, obesity and increased risk of mental health issues.
- Substance use (e.g. cannabis) may impact brain development and can lead to difficulties with learning and delayed development.
- There is a close relationship between substance-related issues and mental illness and some substances may increase the risk of developing certain mental illnesses.
- Excessive drinking combined with drug use, such as methamphetamines (crystal meth, ice), can have very serious consequences for your health or the health and safety of others, and the law (drink/drug driving or criminal offences due to violence).

The Resources section at the end of the book has more details about substance-related issues around the world.

Do you have an issue with substance use?

You may already be aware of substance-related issues in your life but if you are not sure, there are some tools that can help you decide whether you have a problem with substance use and whether or not to seek help. The CAGE test and AUDIT questionnaire are examples.

THE CAGE TEST

C (cut down): Have you ever felt the need to cut down on your substance use?

A (annoyed): Have people annoyed you by criticising your substance use?

G (guilt): Have you ever felt bad about your substance use?

E (eye-opener): Have you ever used substances first thing in the morning to steady your nerves?

If you answered 'yes' to one, then you should think about whether you might have a problem.
If you answered 'yes' to two or more, then you should seek help.

You might also want to look at the AUDIT questionnaire, which is more detailed. It can be found at https://auditscreen.org/.

Sometimes you have to stop and ask yourself some tough questions:

- Are you making excuses for your substance use?
- Are you using substances to forget about your problems?
- Have any financial, legal, medical, family or work problems developed because of using substances?
- Are you in denial about the seriousness of your substance use?

- Are you willing to do almost anything to get hold of the substances?

Treating substance-related issues

Men often seek out some help because there are problems arising from the substance use, such as difficulties at home, school or work, or with the law. These are certainly times to seek help, but it is good to reach out as early as you can, before there are too many negative consequences.

Remember that many men recover from substance-related issues. As with other mental health issues and treatments, no 'one size fits all'. This is because men who use substances vary in what they have used, how long they have used them, how much they have used, where they have used them and other health concerns. As a result, there are many different treatment approaches. You may have a particular preference, so the main thing is to have information about different options.

A general approach is harm minimization or reducing the potential harms associated with substance use (e.g. if you are going to binge drink or take drugs, ensure a sober friend is around, know of needle exchange programs, or pill testing at events). Here is an example of harm minimization with alcohol:

Bob was experiencing ill-health due to excessive alcohol use. With support, he was able to reduce his alcohol intake from at least one bottle a day to four glasses, then down to two, and finally one glass on most days. His general health improved as a result.

The aim of treatment is recovery, or the process of improved physical, psychological and social wellbeing and health. However, only a small proportion of men struggling with substance-related issues commit to treatment. There can be barriers including denial that there is a problem, having access to information about treatment options, or money for treatment. Motivation can be key to getting help and attending treatment. It is made up of the desire to change, confidence in being able to do so, and making it a priority in life.

Working with motivation

The basis of most treatments is working with motivation. To understand motivation, you need to recognize there is a process in overcoming substance use, which is based on the 'stages of change' model. Think about quitting smoking for a moment. Look at the model on the following page and see how a man may be at various stages in readiness to quit: he may not be thinking of quitting at all, he may be planning to quit, or he may be at the stage of quitting altogether.

There are some therapies that can help you to harness your motivation. They include 'motivational interviewing' and 'motivational enhancement therapy' (see the Resources section at the end of the book). You may want to seek out alcohol and drug specialists or counsellors who are experienced in these. In the meantime, try the following exercise to see what level of motivation you have.

TEN QUESTIONS TO MOTIVATE CHANGE

1. What difficulties have you had in relation to your substance use?
2. What is there about your substance use that you or other people might see as reasons for concern?
3. What worries you about your substance use? How do you feel about it?
4. What do you think will happen if you don't make a change?
5. What are the reasons you see for making a change? What are some reasons for not making a change?
6. What might be some good things about making a change? How might this alter your life for the better?
7. If you were 100 per cent successful and things worked out exactly as you wished, what would be different?
8. What makes you think that if you did decide to make a change, you could do it?
9. What do you think would work for you, if you decided to change? What would help you get 'unstuck'?
10. On a scale of 1 to 10, where 1 is not ready to change and 10 is ready to change right now, where are you at the moment? What would need to happen to get you from the lower number to a higher one?

Sometimes it can help to weigh up the pros and cons of *using* the substance by making lists. Be careful to be realistic about the pros and cons. Examples with smoking cigarettes might be: 'It helps me to relax' (pro) or 'my kids want me to quit' (con). You can also do a table for the pros and cons of *not* using the substance.

PROS AND CONS OF SUBSTANCE USE	
Pros	**Cons**

You might find these general tips to improve motivation useful (and they might help you deal with cravings too — more on this later).

TIPS TO INCREASE MOTIVATION

- Focus on your values — what is really important to you?
- Set one goal and then plan steps to work towards your goal.
- Tell others about your plans and get their support.

- Remember the pros and cons. What will you gain from doing this?
- Stop unhelpful habits and create some new, more helpful ones.
- Acknowledge your success, no matter how small!
- Be aware of unhelpful thoughts or uncomfortable feelings, and deal with them (see chapters 3, 4 and 7).
- Be your own coach and encourage yourself via your thoughts.
- Visualize your success.
- Choose a role model and act like them.
- Take action!

For your recovery, it is important to have a treatment program tailored to your particular needs. Ultimately, you want to end up with your toolkit full of approaches that work for you. Depending on how severe the issues are, a range of treatments may be advised:

- Self-help guides can help, such as those produced by drug and alcohol services or different government agencies. You will find that there is information available for men from different cultural backgrounds. (See an example of self-help tips for cutting down alcohol on page 148).
- Phone-counselling services from local drug and alcohol services.
- Supervised withdrawal/medical withdrawal programs which may be done at home or in a treatment facility.
- Individual psychological treatment with a therapist, or in a group, exploring the reasons for substance use

and how to develop new behaviours and skills, such as problem-solving or communication skills (so you develop the confidence and skills to say no to alcohol or drugs, for example, or feel more confident when out in social situations).

- Treatment of any related mental health problems, such as depression, or other issues such as gambling.
- Medications to reduce cravings or to replace a dangerous drug with a safer drug.
- Lifestyle measures to improve what you are eating, your sleep or exercise, for example. Refer back to Chapter 2 for more information on lifestyle, especially stress management. Try to do more of the activities you enjoy that are not related to substance use.
- Maintenance treatment to prevent relapse via step programs or support groups.
- Relapse prevention planning (more on this later) and accepting that relapse is not the end of the world.
- Social supports (e.g. housing or financial support) and growing more social connections (e.g. with family or friends, or community groups).
- Assistance for family or carers, providing information, support or advice about being consistent and avoiding enabling the substance use problem.
- Residential rehabilitation. For some men who have not been able to cease their substance use despite working with a variety of other treatments, more intensive 'in-house' residential rehabilitation programs might be needed.

Abstinence and 'controlled substance use'

Most people experiencing substance-related issues grapple with whether they should cease the substance completely or just cut down (called 'controlled substance use'). The idea of completely stopping may be too extreme, but they would like to regain control over their substance use. Research shows that the more dependent the person is on the substance, the more likely that cutting down or controlled substance use will not be successful.

When a man is dependent on a substance, ceasing completely is the best option. There is a possibility that returning to controlled substance use, such as having one drink at a family social event, after a long period of abstinence will be sustainable. However, many men, once they have re-established a life without alcohol or drug use, are reluctant to risk going back to drinking or using, even on rare occasions.

KEY POINT

The more dependent the person is on the substance, the more likely that 'controlled substance use' will not be successful. For someone who is dependent, stopping use completely is the best option.

For those individuals who are not heavily dependent but do want to cut down to safer or less risky levels of drinking, here is an example of a self-help guide for reducing alcohol consumption.

TEN TIPS FOR CUTTING DOWN ON ALCOHOL

1. Monitor your drinking habits. Keep a diary of how much and how often you drink.
2. Change your drinking habits. Set some goals, such as not drinking alone or when stressed. Schedule at least two alcohol-free days each week.
3. Don't drink on an empty stomach (a full stomach slows the absorption of alcohol).
4. Quench your thirst with water, rather than alcohol.
5. Drink slowly. Sip it rather than gulping it and put down the glass after each mouthful.
6. Take a break. Make every second drink a non-alcoholic drink.
7. Buy low-alcohol alternatives (e.g. light beer or reduced alcohol wine).
8. Opt out of 'shouts'. If you can't avoid buying a shout, get yourself a non-alcoholic drink.
9. Avoid salty snacks, as salt makes you thirsty and more inclined to drink fast.
10. Do something other than drink (e.g. play a game of darts or pool). You're less likely to drink if you're busy doing something.

Psychological approaches

Cognitive behaviour therapy, mindfulness, interpersonal and family therapy, and solution-focused therapy (a therapy focusing on potential solutions, such as using your strengths and identifying tools used in the past and using them again) are all approaches that can help with substance-related issues. Another model called 'dialectical behaviour therapy' may also be used. It can help engage men in therapy and stay in treatment longer and manage uncomfortable emotions (see Chapter 6).

You might like to read the information on cognitive behaviour therapy in chapters 3 and 4 again so you are familiar with the approach. Behaviours such as staying away from situations associated with substance use (e.g. not going to a bar or learning to manage cravings) are part of therapy. Remember that when you stop using the substance, cravings will reduce over time. Some men find keeping a record of urges useful, or they use the 'surf an urge' technique outlined on page 67. Here is an example of a diary to manage urges or cravings for substance use.

URGES DIARY

Date/ time	Situation (where, with whom)	Strength of urge to use (1 to 10)	Feelings (e.g. angry, worried)	Thoughts	Outcomes (how you challenged your thoughts or the actions you took (e.g. left situation))	How did you feel after?
Saturday 11 p.m.	At John's gathering	8	Anxious	'I don't fit in any more!'	'That is just a thought, these are my friends.'	Calmer, urge down to 4

Strategies for managing impulses (acting on something you want immediately) will be needed. We don't come into life with good impulse control; it needs to be learnt. Impulse control involves:

1. Setting things up to reduce triggers. Think about the areas of your life which give you trouble, such as particular places or times (e.g. when stressed or anxious). Do some planning around how to remove access to any substances that cause problems, such as avoiding gatherings where drugs are available, and spending more time with people who are not using substances.

2. Responding when you get caught out. If you find yourself in a situation where there is temptation, try counting to 10 (or more), and breathing. Look back at the tips to increase motivation as some of these might also be helpful. And remind yourself of why you are not wanting to use the substances, even write yourself a note about them. You might also want to recruit some support from trusted family or friends.

The following 'coping with cravings' list incorporates many of the ideas we have just covered. You could type up the list onto a card and put it in your wallet!

COPING WITH CRAVINGS
- Avoid high-risk situations.
- Remove temptations and triggers.
- The urge to use lasts for short periods of time and will pass. If you have a craving, wait an hour (or two or three) before acting on it. You can 'surf the urge' too (see page 67).
- Other things you can do are: watch a movie, clean the house, meditate, see a friend, have a nap or a glass of water, go on the internet, call a friend or family member, pat the dog or cat, chew some gum, do a crossword puzzle, do some exercise.

- Remember your 'why'; that is, why you wanted to stop using and what will happen if you go back to using.
- Call a friend or support agency.

Therapy can also involve noticing your thoughts before using substances (e.g. 'I can't stand the cravings' or 'a bit won't hurt'). You can learn to challenge these thoughts using questions such as:

- What is the evidence that this thought is true?
- Is there another way to think about it?
- What is the worst/best possible outcome?
- If I am honest with myself, what is the most likely outcome?
- What should I do about the situation?
- What is the effect of believing this thought?
- What might happen if I change my thinking?
- If a friend was in this situation and having this thought, what would I say to him/her? [9]

We looked at the idea of underlying or core beliefs in Chapter 3. Negative beliefs that may influence your thinking and behaviours related to substance use might include: 'I am unlovable' or 'I am not good enough.' Unhelpful thoughts, such as really self-critical ones, can come from these underlying beliefs.

It is important to work with these core beliefs when there is substance use. For example, when you have stopped using the substance a situation might trigger these beliefs and a range of unhelpful thoughts and feelings might follow, such as meeting a past friend who is very successful in their business, which might trigger a belief such as 'I am not good enough.' The resultant thoughts might be 'I am such a failure,' with feelings like disappointment or anger. These beliefs and spiralling thinking patterns may trigger substance use and so need to be worked on (see Resources section at the end of the book).

You may also find therapies based around mindfulness helpful, such as acceptance and commitment therapy, which helps you to focus on your values, use your strengths, and be more aware of your thoughts and feelings. In the process it helps your mind to be more connected to the moment, to be more flexible and resilient.

Go back to the section on acceptance and commitment therapy in chapters 3 and 4, to see how it encourages acceptance of thoughts and feelings, no matter how distressing they might be. It talks about defusion, a tool which enables you to observe your thoughts and feelings and to be with them (rather than trying to avoid them). An essential defusion technique to have in your toolkit is 'Sitting with emotion' (see page 84).

We all need to learn to soothe uncomfortable thoughts and feelings in healthy ways. Substances may seem to help you avoid or numb these feelings, but the substances come with negative consequences. The more tools you have to self-soothe, the better. A whole range are outlined in Chapter 6, so take some time to have a look at them.

Relapse prevention

The importance of preventing relapse has been talked about on page 130. In substance use there can be shame when a relapse occurs, as it might be viewed as 'weakness'. But overcoming substance use is very challenging. It is not weak to have had the courage to make changes or to tackle a slip. Nor is it the end of the world.

It is particularly important to be aware of high-risk situations for relapse (e.g. being stressed or being in certain social situations), and to have a plan for preventing issues, such as avoiding the situation or contacting a friend for some support.

STEPS TO TAKE WHEN THERE IS A RELAPSE IN SUBSTANCE USE

1. 'Stop, look and listen.' This helps you to interrupt what is happening.
2. Make a plan for recovery. Call someone, remove yourself from the situation, make an appointment, use the tools that have helped before.
3. Stay calm and breathe, remind yourself you are safe.
4. Tap into your commitment to make changes (refer back to your answers to the 'Ten questions to motivate change' exercise on page 143).
5. Review the situation leading up to the relapse and see what you can do differently.
6. Keep using supports.
7. Work through any troublesome thoughts or feelings (e.g. guilt, anger).[10]

You may need to revisit your cognitive behaviour therapy tools again. There are also some useful websites such as SMART Recovery which has useful information about relapse or 'back-sliding' (see the Resources section at the end of the book).

GAMBLING

Most people in the western world gamble at some stage, and some will develop problems with it. In North America, about 2.2 million adults (1.2 per cent) have a problem with gambling, and many more are at risk.[11] Australians gamble about $20 billion per year, with slot machine gambling being the biggest contributor. It is thought that only about 1 in 8 people struggling with gambling actually seek help.[12]

It has only been in the last twenty years or so that the idea of addiction has been applied to problems like gambling (including internet gambling). The same reward system as in substance use (dopamine) is switched on in the brain. Gambling and substance use share many features, such as building tolerance or needing to do more of the behaviour to get the same satisfaction.

Men tend to start gambling at an earlier age than women, and the problem often arises in adolescence (when the brain has more activity with dopamine). Gambling often occurs when there is depression, anxiety or substance-related issues. It can be a way of avoiding uncomfortable feelings and lessening feelings of anxiety or depression. If gambling is a significant issue, some of the following features will be present:

- Needing to gamble with increasing amounts of money.
- Being restless or irritable when attempting to cut down on gambling.
- Repeatedly failing in efforts to reduce gambling.
- Often being preoccupied with gambling.
- Often gambling when feeling distressed.
- After losing, often returning to chase losses.
- Lying to conceal the extent of gambling.
- Risking or losing significant relationships, jobs or educational opportunities.
- Relying on other people to provide money because of financial problems.[13]

Gambling can have a major effect on relationships, families, work and finances, as well as on a person's sense of self-worth and mental health. The most important aspect of recovery is to recognize that there is a problem and to ask for help. There can be a lot of shame and stigma to overcome with a gambling addiction. There are organizations in the community with expertise, as well as professionals who specialize in the area. It is vital to treat any related issues, such as trauma, depression or anxiety, when addressing a gambling addiction.

KEY POINT

Gambling can have a major effect on all aspects of life, including health and wellbeing. It is vital to recognize that there is a problem and to ask for help.

There are self-help resources available (see Resources section at the end of the book), and it can be useful to join a support group. Increasing your own social connections and supports is also recommended. Do more activities that you are interested in that relieve stress, get rid of credit cards and seek financial counselling if need be (see Chapter 3).

Approaches that can assist are 'motivational interviewing' (see the Resources section at the end of the book) and cognitive behaviour therapy. Depending on the individual, the focus may be on behaviours related to seeking pleasure, on beliefs around being able to control random events, or exposing particular cues related to gambling (e.g. the sounds or visual cues of slot machines) to lessen the urge to gamble.

The strategies to manage urges covered in the last section

on substance use may assist. Postponing gambling, distracting yourself and using relaxation tools are recommended. Visualizing the outcome of gambling on your finances or your family may act as a deterrent. The key to recovery is learning to manage emotions that are uncomfortable (see Chapter 6).

PORNOGRAPHY ADDICTION

Pornography has been around for a long time in different formats. Some people aren't interested in it, and some are very offended by it. Some use it occasionally for the purpose of sexual arousal, while others use it regularly. It has become much easier to access since the internet, and having constant access makes it more difficult to stop using it. Occasional use of pornography may not be a problem, but addiction can become a major issue. Although not formally recognized as an addiction, the American Society of Addiction Medicine (ASAM) recognizes it as a health issue.

Addiction and 'compulsive' behaviours can be the drivers to excessive use of pornography. Compulsions are repeated behaviours, often to relieve anxiety, while addiction involves an inability to stop the behaviour despite negative consequences. Either way, some men find using pornography becomes a behaviour they struggle to control. This can impact relationships, sexual satisfaction, work and self-worth.

The reasons for this will vary. Viewing pornography may start during a period when you feel bored, lonely, anxious or depressed. You may start looking at porn because you like it, or you may enjoy the rush it gives you and then find yourself wanting that rush more and more. Your porn habits may start to cause you problems or you may feel bad about it, but it's the high that you cannot resist. If you try to stop, you may find you cannot. It is probably the same brain mechanism as substance use that is involved — the release of dopamine.

Pornography may be a cause for concern if you:

- find that the amount of time you spend watching porn keeps growing
- feel as though you need a porn 'fix', and that fix gives you a 'high'
- feel guilty about the consequences of viewing porn
- spend hours looking at online porn sites, even if it means neglecting responsibilities or sleep
- insist that your partner views porn or acts out porn fantasies even though they don't want to, or
- are unable to enjoy sex without first viewing porn or are unable to resist porn even though it's disrupting your life.[14]

TIPS TO REGAIN CONTROL OVER PORN VIEWING:

- Delete electronic porn and bookmarks from all of your devices.
- Discard all your hard-copy porn.
- Have someone else install anti-porn software on your electronic devices without giving you the password.
- Plan another activity or two that you can turn to when the urge to view porn hits.
- When you want to view porn, remind yourself how it has affected your life.
- Consider if there are any triggers and try to avoid them.
- Get some help from a trusted friend who will ask about your porn habit and hold you accountable.

- Keep a journal to track progress and any setbacks (remember they are just setbacks and to keep going).[15]

You may also decide that you need to see a therapist for extra help. If you are not keen on seeing a therapist face to face, search for one who will do online or phone therapy. Support groups are also available, and it is again important to focus on a healthy lifestyle. Regularly exercising, meditating, and socializing can make the therapy work faster and decrease the chance of a relapse.

Therapy addressing porn addiction may focus on issues around shame, denial, loneliness or fear of intimacy. There may be co-existent mental health issues such as anxiety, depression or schizophrenia, which are contributing to the problem. And men often become addicted to pornography because it allows them to escape into fantasies rather than coping with reality. Porn is also a distraction that enables you to put off dealing with problems or uncomfortable emotions (see Chapter 6).

Therapists who treat clients for porn addiction commonly use cognitive behaviour therapy to address any underlying beliefs or thoughts linked to the addiction. Therapy also aims to help you understand how excessive use of pornography is preventing you from living a full and healthy life in relation to sex, intimacy and relationships.[16] Together you work out goals to gradually reduce or stop porn use.

ADDICTION TO TECHNOLOGY

Technology is fabulous, but it is a problem when there is compulsive use. Research suggests that many individuals spend more than 46 hours per week looking at screens and, on average, check their smartphones about 85 times a day. [17] Laws are now being passed around the world related to phone use while driving, or for pedestrians on screens due to rising traffic accidents.

Technology addiction may be related to:

- Virtual relationships via social media, dating apps, texting or messaging, rather than having relationships with real people. If you spend less time with real people than in the virtual world, there may be a problem.
- Compulsive web searching, watching videos or checking sites, causing you to neglect other aspects of your life.
- Cybersex addiction with hours spent on pornography, sexting or adult-messaging, impacting negatively on your life.
- Online compulsions such as gaming or shopping, which can cause many financial or social issues.[18]

KEY POINT

You'll know you are addicted to technology when you spend a lot of time on your device, causing you to neglect people, work or other important aspects of your life. Or if you respond with anxiety and distress to a request to 'go for a period of time without it'.

In 2018, the World Health Organization included gaming addiction (digital or video) on a list of diagnosable conditions. They said, however, that only a small proportion of gamers would be diagnosed as 'addicted'. The fact that tablets or smartphones can be taken anywhere means that compulsions can readily be acted on. There is actually a name for smartphone addiction — nomophobia — which is the fear of being without a mobile device or smartphone!

Again, the release of dopamine in the brain is related to technology use, and tolerance can be developed so that increasing amounts of time on the device are needed to give the same pleasure response. Technology addiction can result in:

- Worsening stress, anxiety, loneliness and depression.
- Reduced attention and concentration due to the constant stream of stimulation overwhelming the brain.
- Reduced ability to think deeply or creatively, to remember and learn.
- Sleep disturbances.
- Being more self-absorbed.

Signs you might be addicted to technology include sneaking off to use a device, lying about how much time you are using it, getting irritable when your time is interrupted, or feeling panicky when you leave your smartphone or device somewhere and are without it. Another sign is being 'fearful of missing out' (FOMO) on something that's going on online (e.g. on social media). Remember that we have been taught that we are inadequate by advertising over the years, so naturally we fight against this, and potentially missing out on things buys into this idea. 'The fear of missing out has become pervasive in society. Teens and adults text while driving, because the possibility of a social connection is more important than their own lives (and the lives of others).'[19] So, what are the options for managing this addiction?

- Get support from family, friends or a therapist.

- Recognize the triggers such as boredom or stress. Are you using the device to soothe anxiety or when feeling down?
- Get treatment for any underlying issues, such as depression or trauma.
- Work on your coping skills (e.g. managing stress, sitting with uncomfortable emotions (see Chapter 6).
- Accept that you can't keep up with everything that's going on online.
- Find people to interact with (we need face-to-face social connection) through social or sporting clubs, meet-up groups or classes.
- And don't forget that your children will imitate you, so aim to be a role model to them!

Given you are probably going to cut back on the use of the device rather than get rid of it, some tips to help you to limit your use of the device may be helpful. Alex has put a list together.

TIPS ON HOW TO LIMIT THE USE OF YOUR DEVICE

- Work out a goal (e.g. cutting back the time spent by only using the device at certain times of day).
- Keep a log of how much time you are spending on your devices and look at any patterns of use.
- Turn off the device when you need/want to concentrate on something else (e.g. when driving, talking with a friend, working, playing with children).
- Have device-free places such as the bedroom.

- Replace use of the device with other activities (e.g. exercise, reading, talking with a friend).
- Remove some social media apps from your phone.
- Limit the number of times you check your device.

If you need assistance, consider seeing a therapist or seek out a support group. With gaming addictions, there are now residential programs in some places. Relapse prevention is important, and the same principles apply as in substance use (see page 130). If the behaviour re-occurs work out a new plan, start again and keep trying.

WHAT WE HAVE LOOKED AT SO FAR!

Substance-related issues and addictions are very common. The same mechanism in the brain (dopamine and endorphins) operates with all addictions, whether it's related to substance use, excessive gambling, pornography or technology.

The main thing is to recognize that there is a problem, and to do something about it. There may be many reasons for the problem, including mental health issues such as anxiety or depression. But excessive use creates many new problems. It is important to consider some key points on substance use.

KEY POINTS ON SUBSTANCE USE

- We know that young people model their behaviour on adults. If you don't want your children to drink or use other substances, then reduce or stop yourself.

- The later people use a substance, the less likelihood there is that they will run into problems with them.
- There's actually no safe level of alcohol consumption. Men are much more likely than women to experience or cause injury as a result of substance use.
- If there's a family history of substance use disorder or mental health issues, then you need to be very cautious about any alcohol or drug use.
- Staying in school and finding employment will protect against substance-related issues.
- Communities need to look at developing a range of after-hours alcohol- and smoking-free activities, especially for younger males. For example, some countries have access to sporting, arts and other recreational activities and facilities as a way of reducing substance use.
- Be aware of the risk for men of developing alcohol problems at a later age, maybe triggered by loss or grief (retirement, loss of partner), and seek help.
- Be aware of changing patterns of drinking and seek help early.
- Learn how to manage stress, cravings and impulses.

(Thank you to Dr Chris Holmwood for highlighting these key messages.)

A key risk factor in substance use and various addictions is difficulty expressing emotions and self-medicating when there are uncomfortable feelings. Being socially isolated, in poverty, or not having a range of coping skills or meaningful activities in life are also risk factors.

Remember Tim from earlier this chapter? Struggling with substance-related issues and gambling, Tim sought help from a doctor on the advice of his parents.

Tim went to see a doctor and a therapist who identified a number of significant issues including anxiety in social situations, worry about being accepted by friends and gaining his father's approval. Tim also struggled to manage his emotions, such as anger, and his self-confidence was very low.

Tim engaged on and off with therapy, in which the focus was on cognitive behaviour therapy, schema therapy, tolerating distressing emotions and building self-confidence.

He was encouraged by his doctor and family to abstain from substance use and gambling. He had some relapses, but over time mostly managed to abstain by focusing on his fitness and work.

His family helped with his financial problems and organized for Tim to see a financial counsellor. Tim reconnected with some friends who did not engage in substance use and met a new girlfriend.

Tim's story highlights that there is help available and change is always possible. There are a range of psychological approaches that can help with motivation, support and practical tools to assist you to regain control over the issue. Remember that 'no one size fits all', so look at what is available and decide what's best for you, and that many men overcome the issues with some help.

The main thing is to recognize when substance use (including alcohol) or other activities are becoming more and more important in your life. Think about what you want in life and 'why' and take steps to do something about the problem. Learning a range of coping skills that you can have in your toolkit is key. These will be helpful for the rest of your life.

6.

DEALING WITH UNCOMFORTABLE FEELINGS (SUCH AS ANGER AND GRIEF)

You have power over your mind — not outside events.
Realize this, and you will find strength.

Marcus Aurelius

We have already spoken about men being taught by society that it is 'not okay' to express a range of emotions. For this reason, this chapter is one of the most important in the book, as it focuses on dealing with uncomfortable emotions. Sometimes you will feel terrific in life and experience emotions like joy, excitement and happiness. At other times you will be really uncomfortable, when experiencing feelings like shame, anger, sadness or disappointment.

There are actually no 'good' or 'bad' emotions because they are all giving us information to help us co-operate with others and to survive. We don't need to fear feelings or not talk about them. However, some feelings just don't feel great and we tend to try to avoid these, which can lead to more problems.

Professor Andrew Reimer recently spoke about boys and young men needing to be given the language of emotions, and permission for emotional honesty. He also said that anger is the only culturally acceptable emotion for males to show.[1]

We know that assisting men to express themselves more freely will help prevent mental health issues. This process is about developing 'emotional intelligence' or being able to recognize and manage your emotions. We will look at this further later in the book.

As author Jack Kornfield said, 'You can't stop the waves, but you can learn to surf!' This chapter is all about managing the more challenging 'waves' of emotions: shame, guilt, anger, loss and grief. These are the ones that most commonly seem to come up in therapy, and we will go through a range of practical approaches to help you with them.

GUILT AND SHAME

The emotions of guilt and shame have already been introduced in Chapter 1 and, in particular, that shame is a major barrier to acknowledging there is a mental health issue and getting some help. Shame is often hidden. Returning to the work of Brené Brown, when she asked men what 'shame' meant to them, they said 'failure (whether) at work, on the sporting field, in marriage or in bed'. It meant 'being wrong or defective in some way'. It also meant 'showing fear' or other people thinking you are 'soft', which was thought of as being degrading.

Brown says that men are socialized to project being great and powerful, no matter how they feel or how hard they are working on the inside. They experience shame when this exterior is threatened. It is disempowering for men and can include embarrassment, guilt and self-consciousness. It may be related to being rejected or feeling disappointed. And you can experience shame from a mild level to a very intense level. Some useful definitions of guilt and shame (from Brené Brown) are as follows:

- Shame involves a focus on self, with thoughts like, 'I am bad' or 'I am a mistake', meaning that there is something 'inherently wrong with who I am'. It is the opposite of pride.
- Guilt relates to behaviours or actions, with related thoughts such as, 'I did something bad' or 'I made a mistake'.[2]

Shame can be related to depression and suicide, trauma, addictions and violence, whereas guilt is not. Shame is said to be so uncomfortable for men that often it comes into therapy in 'disguise' as low self-esteem, eating issues or social anxiety.[3]

Men naturally want to be 'one of the boys', and so they measure themselves up to other males. The trap is thinking that you are 'not good enough', which can lead to a sense of being disconnected from yourself, being self-critical, feeling insecure, setting unrealistic expectations or being aggressive.

Shame is also related to underlying human needs for love and belonging, to know we matter and that we are part of something. We try to fit in to what society tells us to do and it is extremely painful when we don't think we measure up or are not worthy.

Shame is just as relevant for gay men as for straight men, but there are concerns unique to gay men. The statement, 'Be a man' is particularly degrading. If a gay man has a sense of being an outsider in society, shame will heighten this.[4]

KEY POINT

Shame is a barrier to dealing with any mental health issues. Men are socialized to project being powerful, no matter how they feel. They experience shame when this exterior is threatened and it is disempowering for them.

There are some potential solutions to issues with guilt and shame and regaining a sense of empowerment. These include:

- being aware of the issues and putting words to the feelings
- working through shame rather than avoiding it
- developing more understanding of emotions such as the difference between guilt and shame
- developing empathy
- working with your thoughts.

FEELING MORE EMPOWERED

Take a moment to reflect on how you might work with these 'solutions' to reduce any sense of shame and to feel more empowered. Write down your ideas, including any other ones you come up with.

Brown talks about developing 'shame resilience' or learning to tolerate it. To do this we have to make ourselves vulnerable in a culture that tells men 'to man up' and demands perfection in many ways. Examples of making yourself vulnerable are admitting you are struggling, saying you are afraid, or even saying 'I don't know'. Remember that making yourself vulnerable does not mean weakness; it can be an act of courage and can deepen our connection to others (see the Resources section at the end of the book).

Let's have a look at a few tips that may be helpful in dealing with guilt and shame.

TIPS FOR DEALING WITH GUILT AND SHAME

- Name your feelings.
- Make a decision to work on guilt or shame and make a start.
- Relate to them in a different way; step back from them and take a look at them.
- Explore feelings of guilt or shame courageously. Read about them, talk or write about them, or see a therapist to explore their origins.
- Be honest with yourself about shame in particular, rather than running from it or denying it.
- Remember that you are not the guilt or shame (i.e. they do not represent your whole identity).
- Take a look at your head talk. Is it self-critical? Reframe it into something more positive (e.g. 'Everyone makes mistakes, you're doing okay!').
- Be compassionate towards yourself (see page 110), and sometimes forgive yourself.
- Connect with other people and focus on empathy (being able to step into someone else's shoes).
- Understand that no one is perfect and do some work on perfectionism (see page 117).
- Deal with any fear stemming from guilt or shame (e.g. being anxious socially or not going for a particular job).
  Identify any triggers to shame (e.g. criticism about work or being a parent).

- Use humour when these emotions pop up (sometimes smile or laugh at yourself).
- Focus on your strengths (see page 43) as well as meaningful activity and purpose.
- Learn from your efforts and keep making changes.

ANGER

Anger can be a normal, healthy reaction to feeling threatened and is part of your 'fight–flight–freeze' or survival response. It can also follow on from feeling scared, sad, hurt, insecure or lonely. And having a blast of anger is a release that makes men feel powerful versus feeling vulnerable.

It has been reported that more men in western countries are presenting to therapists because of anger issues,[5] and information from over 24,000 young people aged twelve to 25 indicates that anger-related problems are one of the main issues among this age group seeking help. Only depression and anxiety ranked higher.[6]

Men's roles and work options are changing in life, and this is said to be a contributor to anger. Anger can also be an issue when there is co-existing depression or substance use. Other factors that can contribute to men feeling angry are stress, frustration (e.g. work, sexual), being tired, hungry or in pain, grief or physical withdrawal from certain drugs.

Anger changes the brain. Remember the limbic system in the brain, which houses the amygdala or emotional centre (see page 37)? This part of the brain registers something like fear or rejection and triggers the fight–flight–freeze response and loads of stress hormones are released into the body. These reduce activity in the brain cortex, which is responsible for making decisions and judgement. This is why it can be hard to make good decisions when feeling angry.

KEY POINT

Men are seeking help more often for issues with anger. This may relate to managing changes in life or underlying mental health issues. Anger changes the brain and these changes make it harder for men to make good decisions.

Anger can range from feeling frustrated or annoyed to full-blown rage, and rage can lead to unreasonable or violent actions (because you are not thinking clearly in this state). Anger becomes a problem when it impacts negatively on relationships, work, health or causes issues with the law. Signs that it is a problem include:

- The anger involves verbal, emotional, physical or psychological abuse (including domestic violence).
- You feel angry a lot of the time.
- People are worried about your anger.
- The anger is leading to problems with relationships or work.
- The anger is out of proportion to the triggering event(s) or lasts a long time.
- It is causing anxiety, depression, or triggering substance use.

Potential benefits of learning to manage anger are improved health and wellbeing, reduced risk of harm to oneself and others, increased self-confidence, improved relationships and better quality of life. Anger will always be one of your range of feelings, so it is not a matter of getting rid of it but changing how you use it and outgrowing any dysfunctional behaviours. For men, 'Managing anger can be closely tied to working out how they "do" their emotions and learning how to "do" them differently. This means having a good look at themselves and working out how they "work"; this is often tied in with other issues, around childhood and early experiences which can drive how we all behave.'[7]

Men experiencing anger issues may believe that their anger is not their fault. This can lead them to blame everyone else. Admitting that there's a problem, despite shame often being present, is the first step in dealing with anger issues. Deciding to get help is the next big step. As we have talked about, reaching out can be hard as it means making yourself vulnerable. Unfortunately, at times it is only when there is a crisis that men reach out.

There are many tips and tools for learning to tame anger. Not all will fit for you, depending on how much of an issue anger is for you. However, it is important to heed psychiatrist Viktor Frankl's words: 'Between *stimulus and response* there is a space. In that space is our power to choose our response. In our response *lies our growth and our freedom.*' To make use of this 'space', see the following exercise.

WHEN YOU NOTICE ANGER IS CLOSE
- Say 'stop!' loudly in your mind, then count to 20 before you respond.
- Maybe take some time out (e.g. leave the room for a few minutes to cool down).[8]

And here are some general tips for taming anger that Alex has come up with. It can be something that takes some practice.

TIPS FOR TAMING ANGER

- Try to understand your anger (maybe through talking or writing about it).
- Keep a diary of when your anger is occurring and note any triggers that are setting it off.
- Identify and name any related feelings, such as hurt or shame, and deal with them.
- Take responsibility for changing unhealthy behaviours.
- Question whether you are actually angry with yourself and putting this onto someone else.
- Identify signs of anger (e.g. breathing more quickly, feeling tense in the muscles).

Take a few moments to process the tips above, then go onto the next group of tips!

- Only express anger in a way that fits with who you want to be.
- Look at other ways to express anger (e.g. exercise, talking, working in the shed).
- Do some regular relaxation or mindfulness (see chapters 2 and 3).
- Think about healthy boundaries or limits (your own and other people's).
- Use problem-solving to sort out issues.
- Let go of the idea that you can control other people.

- When angry, delay speaking until you are calm. Communicate about the problem rather than getting angry; listen and ask questions.
- Develop helpful self-talk (e.g. 'stay calm, relax and breathe easy; I can do this').
- Develop empathy by working on understanding the other person's viewpoint.
- Use distraction (e.g. listen to music, do a manual task such as washing the car).
- Don't sweat the small stuff! Ask yourself, 'How important is this? Is it worth getting angry about?'
- Use humour to reduce the tension.
- Work on forgiving others more often.
- Remember to practise, and then practise some more!

Well done for working through the tips and we hope that you identified a few that might assist. Remember Tim from earlier? Here is more of his story and the tips and strategies he found helpful.

Anger was a significant issue for Tim. Part of his therapy focused on taking responsibility for changing related behaviours. Tim did not understand his emotions very well and he tended to avoid uncomfortable ones.

In therapy Tim learnt to identify other emotions related to his anger, such as anxiety. He used breathing exercises and worked on his self-talk. He learnt to communicate more with others about his problems before they became big problems, and that humour helps.

In terms of anger and thinking, it can also be useful to identify your anger triggers (i.e. what thoughts and feelings occurred and how you responded to these). Here is an example to explain the process. You can see that the man in the example dealt with conflict with angry behaviour by leaving the situation.

THOUGHTS AND ANGER

Before my anger	Initial thoughts and feelings	Behaviour	What happened afterwards
Partner asked me to let her know what time I would be back home.	She doesn't trust me. I feel very angry.	Stormed out of the house and slammed the door.	She wouldn't speak to me for the rest of the day, and I went to a hotel.

And remember that any thinking errors (especially black-and-white thinking, mind-reading or labelling) can be traps. Work on identifying them and challenging them (see page 74). Unhelpful underlying beliefs can also be drivers of anger (e.g. 'I'm not good enough'). All the tools from cognitive behaviour therapy covered in earlier chapters can help, as can the tools from acceptance and commitment therapy (see chapters 3 and 4). You may find detaching from your thoughts with mindfulness, or learning to sit with anger and defuse it, helpful (see pages 79–84)

It is also important to learn the difference between being assertive and being angry, and perhaps learn some assertiveness skills. Assertiveness means communicating your view or needs in a clear way, without becoming aggressive. It involves respecting yourself and others. It can involve changing the ways in which you relate to people and the behaviours that you use. Being more assertive can be helpful in many situations, such as dealing with annoyances, responding to criticism or turning down requests.

Let's take an example in which you feel your rights are not being taken into account at work. Maybe a colleague is talking over you at meetings and not asking for your views on a job you know a lot about. Assertiveness can help you express your feelings about their behaviours. It is good to acknowledge the other person first by saying something like, 'I appreciate this is a challenging situation,' and then you can go on to use what we call an 'I' statement in a calm and steady way.

CONSTRUCTING AN 'I' STATEMENT

Use these steps to construct your statement:
1. 'I feel ...' (name the feeling)
2. 'When you ...' (state what the unacceptable behaviour is in a non-blaming way)
3. 'Because ...' (explain the effects of the behaviour on you)
4. 'I'd prefer ...' (what you would like to happen!)

The work example might sound like: 'I appreciate this is a challenging situation. I feel disappointed when you don't ask my views on it because I have a lot of knowledge about the area. I'd prefer it if I could have the opportunity to share my views.'

Having read some of the strategies for managing anger, now take a look at your warning signs for anger and potential triggers, if it is relevant to you. Also make a list of the behaviours that you are going to do to reduce the anger.

YOUR ANGER MANAGEMENT STRATEGIES

My anger warning signs:

Potential trigger situations:

Helpful behaviours that I will use (e.g. time out):

Although it may or may not apply to you, we also need to talk about intense anger as it is said to be the main cause of domestic and family violence. We are talking about aggression, which attacks in some way, whereas anger does not. Aggression can take many forms, from defensiveness to intimidation, hostility or violence. There will be more discussion about domestic violence in Chapter 8.

When physical aggression is a problem, there may be personality characteristics at play. When a man has 'antisocial' characteristics, for example, he tends to disregard the rights of others through breaking the law, lying or being aggressive. These characteristics can trigger violence and criminal behaviour. Substance use, especially alcohol, can be involved and treatment needs to target this (see the Resources section at the end of the book for more information).

LOSS AND GRIEF

Let's start this section on loss and grief by reading about Joshua and Kristen's story:

> Joshua and Kristen saw a therapist together. Three months previously they had been excited about the birth of their first baby, but their little boy was stillborn. They were understandably devastated. They spent time cuddling their son, named and dressed him, and there was a funeral. They were supporting each other in coping with their loss and their family was being very helpful. But they were experiencing intense emotions and felt like they were on a rollercoaster.
>
> To work through her grief, Kristen had started to make a book about her pregnancy and the baby and was spending time with her sister and a friend, talking about the baby and her feelings. Joshua was building a special cubby house in honour of their son.

Loss involves separation from something that has meaning to us and to which we feel connected. Grief is the response to loss, and affects many aspects of us (physical, psychological, social, spiritual). There may be loss associated with death or other losses (e.g. loss of a job, divorce). Some losses are anticipated (e.g. losing a relative with terminal cancer), and some are disenfranchised, that is, not well acknowledged in society (e.g. losing someone who suicides).

As you can see from Joshua and Kristen's story, men and women may express or process grief in different ways. As a generalization, males often remain silent and use denial, and control any expression of their emotions. Anger may dominate. They often express the need to be 'strong' and use action (such as sport) to work through their grief, whereas females process grief through talking and expressing emotions.

Grief is experienced in a number of ways, via feelings, physical sensations, thoughts and behaviours. Feelings can include shock, numbness, sadness, anger, guilt, anxiety, loneliness, helplessness, yearning, despair, depression or relief (for the deceased in ending pain). You may have a sense of disbelief or confusion, a sense of hopelessness or unreality. Physical reactions include tiredness, breathing difficulties or muscle weakness. Behaviours can include crying and being restless. You may withdraw from family and friends, or have problems sleeping or eating.

Working through loss and grief takes time. This is because you lose your sense of attachment to the lost person (or pet), which helps you keep a sense of balance (we are going to look more at attachment in Chapter 8). This is why you can experience feelings like being on a rollercoaster. Loss and grief also threaten our beliefs about the world and it takes time to readjust.

Sometimes grief can be complicated because it remains intense and is long-lasting, especially when the loss involves uncertainty or trauma (e.g. result of an accident or crime). Occasionally depression can result or there may be issues related to the trauma (see Chapter 7). In these instances, seeing a doctor and a therapist can help.

Some experts talk about there being 'tasks' or work in grieving, including:

- Accepting the reality of the loss.
- Working through the pain of grief.
- Adjusting to an environment without the lost person or item.
- Emotionally relocating the lost person or item in your life.

- Rebuilding your own life and identity.

To explain the point about relocating the lost person/item in your life, here is an idea which can be useful that relates to having a continuing bond or connection with the person or item that has been lost: you focus on the meaning of the connection. For example, if you lose a parent and they were a great role model to you, you would continue to see them as a role model and tap into the values they taught you.[9]

An extension of this idea is reconstructing meaning, and this can also be helpful in working through grief. An example might be doing something to honour the person. Sportsperson Nick Riewoldt, who lost his sister to a bone marrow disease, set up a charity to raise money to find a cure for the disease.

If you see a therapist, they will:
- Listen to your story.
- Focus on your strengths.
- Provide empathy, support and information.
- Talk about self-care with sleep, eating, mindfulness and keeping to your routines.
- Encourage some grieving time each day (e.g. half-hour to one hour).
- Use various grief counselling approaches, including cognitive behaviour therapy, acceptance and commitment therapy and narrative therapy.
- Encourage you to keep a journal about your experience with grief or a 'memory box' about the person with mementos and pictures, so that you can pull it out and look at it when you choose.
- Monitor your progress and any risk of self-harm (as you are more vulnerable when grieving).

- When you are ready, encourage reconnection with other people and ways to rebuild your identity.

These are the sorts of tools and approaches that Joshua and Kristen found helpful in grieving the loss of their baby (see also the Resources section at the end of the book).

It is also worth mentioning one particular tool from narrative therapy which encourages you to say 'hello again' to the person you are grieving. This involves incorporating into your life what has been lost, for example, holding on to the influence of that person.

SAY HELLO AGAIN!

By saying 'hello again' to your loved one, you can have an ongoing connection with them while still learning to live a life without them being physically present. To help you do this, ask yourself these questions:
- If you were seeing yourself through [deceased's name] eyes now, what would you be noticing about yourself that you could appreciate?
- What difference would it make to how you feel if you were appreciating this in yourself right now?
- What would [deceased's name] have said or done in certain situations?
- Can you see their characteristics in your sibling or child?

TOLERATING EMOTIONAL DISTRESS

We have looked at several emotions that feel uncomfortable and can create distress. Having the skills to cope with these emotions is vital in life. We have looked at various approaches earlier in the chapter, but it is useful to explore some other self-management skills.

In recent years 'dialectical behaviour therapy' has shown itself to be an effective approach with certain mental health issues, including depression, substance-related issues and post-traumatic stress disorder. The name of the therapy refers to both acceptance of self, at the same time as recognizing the need for change. It is particularly useful if there is a struggle with strong emotions or a tendency to react more intensely to a situation than other people. This approach suggests that we have:

1. The 'emotion mind' which acts when feelings are in the driver's seat and control your thoughts and actions (e.g. acting impulsively).
2. The 'reasonable mind' which focuses on logic and ignores feelings.
3. The 'wise mind' which balances both, recognizing and respecting feelings, but reacting in a reasonable, logical way.[10]

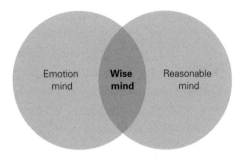

You might recognize these parts of your mind if you think about how you have responded to different experiences in life. An example would be in a situation where you have been criticized. Your 'emotion mind' might have responded with anger or disappointment, whereas the 'reasonable mind' might have recalled events which triggered the criticism. The 'wise mind'

steps back and looks at the situation and your thoughts and feelings, so that you can respond in a considered way. Think about when you have used each part of your mind and how it went!

This therapy contains some very useful ideas in relation to tolerating distress and soothing or regulating emotions. It incorporates taking action aligned with your values (see page 22). This therapy encourages you to connect with valued people, work or spiritual pursuits (if relevant to you) and to practise mindfulness, such as mindfulness relaxation and breathing techniques (see pages 60–62).

And it works from a basis that the more we struggle with and try to avoid distress, the worse it often gets. Some of the ideas from this therapy are helpful for everyone to know. At times we cannot change situations that trigger distress, and we need to work on acceptance or being willing to experience a situation as it is in the moment and without judgement (mindfully).

Dialectical behaviour therapy suggests a whole range of strategies which can help when feeling emotional distress. Some are outlined below.

STRATEGIES TO USE WHEN FEELING DISTRESSED

- Distract from the uncomfortable thought or feelings via any activities you usually engage in (e.g. chores), or enjoy some music, exercise, patting your pet, gardening or watching a film.
- Focus outside of yourself on someone or something else.
- Do something that will create an opposite emotion (e.g. if anxious, listen to calming music; if sad, watch a comedy).
- Push negative thoughts away (e.g. write them on a piece of paper, then crumple them up and throw the paper away) or focus on a pleasant memory instead.
- Focus on other thoughts (e.g. count to ten, read a book).

Identifying and naming feelings is also important in dealing with distress. Using your various senses may help, such as looking at nature around you, listening to music, smelling the fresh air, tasting a soothing tea, or having a shower (touch). Self-care is seen as part of regulating emotions, as eating well, avoiding substances, getting regular exercise and getting enough sleep all help.

Here is another practical strategy to use when emotions are pushing you around. See if you think it would be helpful.

'STOP': TOLERATING DISTRESS
It can help to take a more distant view of the distressing situation or a 'helicopter view' and use STOP:
- Pause, freeze, don't act immediately.
- Take a step back and breathe.
- Observe what is going on around you and inside you (i.e. your thoughts and feelings) and identify the words your mind is saying and ask yourself whether or not they are helpful.
- Put in some perspective by seeing the situation as an outside observer and checking out what they would make of it.
- Proceed mindfully, practise what works for you and do what is appropriate that is most helpful to you (ask your wise mind!).[11]

We have already talked about emotions and actions being closely linked. Dialectical behaviour therapy says every emotion triggers an 'action urge'. When you are anxious, the urge is to avoid. When you are sad, you stop doing things and withdraw. When there is shame, the urge is to defend yourself or hide, and when you are angry, the urge is to fight.[12]

The problem is that these urges can cause more problems, and so one strategy is to take the opposite action!

Dialectical behaviour therapy suggests using problem-solving skills in relation to emotions and perhaps the results of action urges. It involves looking at your thoughts, feelings and actions at each stage of the event and considering what you could have done differently, such as using coping skills or opposite actions.

Finally, it teaches interpersonal skills such as listening to and understanding others, negotiation and assertiveness (see page 176), and dealing with conflict (see Chapter 8).

You might also like to go back and look at some of the ideas from acceptance and commitment therapy, in particular 'Sitting with emotion' (see page 84), which enables you to sit with, and tolerate, distressing feelings.

WHAT WE HAVE LOOKED AT SO FAR!

This has been a really important chapter, given that men are taught to repress their emotions. Our society gives many messages about what it is to be a 'man', and not displaying emotions is one of them. Emotional intelligence involves learning to recognize, name and manage your emotions, and it is good to work on growing this as much as possible (more on this in Chapter 11).

We have looked at shame and guilt, which often generate fear and underlie many mental health issues. More than ever, it is time to learn to drop your defences and allow yourself to be vulnerable. This does not mean being weak but being courageous, and it will open your life to improved relationships and more positive emotions.

Anger is the one emotion men are allowed to express in society. It is a normal emotion, but one that can cause many issues, especially when it impacts your relationships or health. Expressing anger in functional ways is vital, and we have looked at a number of tips and tools that can help.

Loss and grief are also part of life, along with the rollercoaster of emotions that can come with them. There are many approaches and tools that can help you work through loss and grief and realizing the importance of continuing bonds with the lost person or item and finding meaning can be very helpful.

We have also mentioned useful skills to tolerating emotional distress, often generated by emotions. There are strategies to develop the 'wise mind' to help you recognize your feelings and express them in constructive ways. Our suggestion is to read and re-read this chapter and include as many strategies in your toolkit as possible. Learning to deal with uncomfortable emotions will help reduce stress and many other mental health issues and empower you to improve your quality of life.

7.

THE IMPACT OF TRAUMA AND DISASTER ON MEN

When we can talk about our feelings, they become less overwhelming, less upsetting, and less scary. The people we trust with that important talk can help us know that we are not alone.

Fred Rogers

Trauma is probably the most underestimated influence on mental health, and it can have far-reaching and devastating effects. It may result from 'an event, series of events, or set of circumstances experienced by an individual as physically or emotionally harmful or life-threatening with lasting adverse effects on the individual's functioning and ... wellbeing'.[1] Examples of trauma are accidents, assaults or hearing traumatic news about a loved one.

In the USA, 61 per cent of men report exposure to at least one traumatic event and the majority of these have experienced more than one trauma.[2] A study looking at adverse experiences during childhood investigated the impact of a range of traumatic experiences in childhood and found that individuals who had faced trauma in their childhood were at a much greater risk of suicide, eating disorders or substance-related issues.[3]

In this chapter we will look at the causes of trauma for men, the impact of trauma in men's lives and recovery from trauma. But first, have a read of Ben's story, as we will return to it later in the chapter:

> Ben is a 24-year-old soldier. He joined the army at seventeen to leave home and get away from his father who was dependent on alcohol and often violent. Ben was at a local bar with a friend one Friday night, where they had a few drinks. When they went outside to leave, three men confronted them and assaulted them.
>
> Ben was punched in the head and lost consciousness briefly. He was treated at the base and kept in hospital there overnight. In the coming weeks he became irritable and felt on edge all the time. He had nightmares about the assault, and during the day would see it in his mind, over and over. At other times he would also see his father's fist coming towards him.

CAUSES OF TRAUMA FOR MEN

Traumatic events are often unexpected, negative, pose a threat to safety and may be life-threatening. Any event that involves a threat to life or a serious injury has the potential to be traumatic. This includes experiencing natural disasters (more on this later), an accident, and physical or sexual assault. Trauma may occur any time in life, from childhood through to old age. Trauma associated with medical procedures is an example that can impact at any age.

It is important to look at childhood trauma, because adult men may be impacted by earlier life experiences. Childhood trauma may be a single incident or involve repeated physical, verbal or sexual abuse, or physical and emotional neglect. Trauma may occur when a parent abuses alcohol or is diagnosed with a serious mental health issue, or when a parent leaves the family or passes away. Bullying in childhood is also a common cause of trauma.

> ### KEY POINT
>
> Trauma in adult life may be situational, such as experiencing an accident or living through a natural disaster (e.g. bushfires), being assaulted or serving in a war. It can also be due to ongoing abuse (e.g. physical or emotional abuse in a relationship).

Men may witness the trauma, experience it themselves, or it may be that they learn about traumatic events which have occurred to a close family member or friend. An example is receiving news by phone that a parent or child has died suddenly.

THE IMPACT OF TRAUMA

Let's look firstly at what trauma can do to the nervous system, including the brain. Remember our nervous system is wired to respond to threats. Trauma activates the sympathetic arm of the nervous system with the release of various stress hormones (cortisol, adrenaline and norepinephrine), and the following can occur:

- When a man has been affected by trauma, he is likely to have a greater response to any later stress or threat. As a result, a larger amount of stress hormones are released and they have a greater effect on the body, causing symptoms like a rapid heart rate, breathlessness and sweating.

- In a situation where there is trauma, the anxiety can become linked to a trigger. In Ben's assault, one of the men who attacked him was wearing a cap, and Ben developed a fear of other people wearing caps and felt very anxious around them.
- Studies have shown that the brain chemical serotonin is affected in trauma, and this is thought to be why irritability, anger and depression can occur.
- There have been studies on what happens in the brain itself with trauma. Children are particularly at risk because their brain is growing. Their brain may remain in a higher state of stress, affecting them later in life. Refer back to the diagram of the brain on page 37. A child's limbic brain (the amygdala and hippocampus) can be affected. The result may be more extreme emotions and a reduced ability to learn.[4]

You can see that trauma can significantly affect males of all ages. Adult men will respond to trauma in different ways, depending on their past and their personality. And the type and extent of the trauma will have an influence. Remember, too, that men are raised with the ideas that they must be 'tough' and 'soldier on' when there is trauma. What a man tells himself in his mind will have a large impact on how he responds to the trauma.

When trauma occurs, a man may respond with a great deal of distress, often triggered by uninvited memories of the event (e.g. images of an accident), or distressing dreams and flashbacks (reliving the event with images, sounds or smells). With these there can be a sense of loss of reality or actual awareness. The individual may find themselves unable to experience feelings of happiness, for example.

They may also make efforts to avoid any reminders of the trauma and be overly vigilant (the mind scanning for threats), unable to concentrate, or are more irritable or angry. Generally, these feelings often resolve on their own, and with the support of family and friends, the individual recovers.

> A doctor in the air force responded to an aircraft accident in which the pilot was killed. In the few weeks afterwards, his sleep was disturbed, and he felt detached from his partner. He had some flashbacks and a sense of loss of reality at times. Fortunately, the symptoms settled after a few weeks, and there were no ongoing issues.

TIP: In the first days and weeks after a traumatic event, individuals often experience strong emotions and other effects.

In contrast, post-traumatic stress disorder involves the development of long-lasting anxiety following a traumatic event (more than a month). Between 5 and 10 per cent of Australians will suffer from post-traumatic stress disorder at some point in their lives.[5] In the USA, the rate is said to be about 7 per cent.[6] The rates of this disorder are higher in countries with a lot of conflict, or in military personnel compared with the general population (20 to 30 per cent of veterans).[7] Someone with post-traumatic stress disorder has a number of ongoing difficulties:

- Reliving the traumatic event through unwanted memories and sensations (e.g. sounds, smells), vivid nightmares, flashbacks or intense reactions such as heart palpitations or panic when reminded of the event.

- Feeling wound up; that is, having trouble sleeping or concentrating, feeling angry or irritable, taking risks, becoming easily startled, or constantly being vigilant or on the lookout for danger.
- Avoiding reminders of the event, such as activities, places, people, thoughts or feelings that bring back memories of the trauma.
- Uncomfortable thoughts and feelings, including feeling afraid, angry, guilty, depressed or numb a lot of the time, losing interest in day-to-day activities, feeling cut off from friends and family.

You may be interested in a screening tool looking for possible post-traumatic stress disorder. It does not diagnose the disorder (only a doctor or therapist can do this), but it may give you an indication. Then you can follow up with your doctor.

SCREENING TOOL FOR POST-TRAUMATIC STRESS DISORDER

1. Do you avoid being reminded of the experience by staying away from certain places, people or activities?
2. Have you lost interest in activities that were once important or enjoyable?
3. Have you begun to feel more distant or isolated from other people?
4. Do you find it hard to feel love or affection for other people?
5. Have you begun to feel that there is no point in planning for the future?
6. Have you had more trouble than usual falling or staying asleep?

7. Do you become jumpy or easily startled by ordinary noises or movements?

If you answered 'yes' to four or more, a diagnosis of post-traumatic stress disorder is probable and seeking some assistance is recommended (see the Resources section at the end of the book).

You can see how trauma may cause difficulties relating to other people, such as family members or partners, as well as challenges at work. It is also not unusual for people with post-traumatic stress disorder to experience other mental health problems like depression or anxiety. Some men may develop a habit of using substances as a way of coping after trauma.

It is worth being aware of the terms 'complex trauma' or 'complex post-traumatic stress disorder'. This results when multiple traumatic events occur over a period of time (e.g. child abuse, prolonged domestic violence, torture or witnessing genocide). While complex trauma survivors are likely to experience post-traumatic stress disorder, those with complex trauma may have mental health issues such as depression or anxiety, problems with dissociative episodes or psychotic symptoms. Personality and a sense of self-worth can be affected, along with the ability to have stable relationships or to regulate emotions (see the Resources section at the end of the book).

RECOVERY FROM TRAUMA

If you think that trauma is playing a significant role in your life, it is important to seek some help. This can be hard for men to do because of potential barriers, such as seeing themselves as 'weak'.

This idea needs to be challenged. Remember Ben from earlier? Here is more of his story:

> Ben had a review appointment with the doctor a few weeks later. When the doctor asked how he was going, Ben was hesitant, and the doctor encouraged him to talk about what was going on for him. Ben said that he was feeling exhausted by the dreams and disturbed sleep, and worried about what he was experiencing. He was scared that he was 'going to lose it'.
>
> The doctor explained to him that the recent assault and the trauma that he had experienced in his childhood were triggering most of the symptoms, and that he was being courageous to talk about his concerns. They talked more that day and Ben felt a bit calmer after sharing his concerns and saw that what the doctor had said made sense.
>
> The doctor did a physical check-up and discussed the benefits of getting some psychological support for the trauma. The doctor organized for Ben to see one of the therapists on base who had a lot of experience helping soldiers with the effects of trauma. He also scheduled another appointment for Ben to keep an eye on how things were going.

It is important that a good assessment is done, and that any other mental health issues are picked up. Equally, a therapist who knows about the treatment of trauma-related issues needs to be located. It may be that help from a psychiatrist is also needed.

TIP: Make sure you work with doctors and therapists who have experience in the treatment of trauma. Ask your doctor for a referral to professionals with expertise in the area. Websites for different professional organizations often have lists of members and their areas of interest or expertise.

Therapists will generally take a 'trauma-informed approach', meaning they realize the widespread effects of trauma, recognize the symptoms and respond with empathy as much as possible (stepping into your shoes), as well as creating a sense of safety. This way a high level of trust is established, and this is vital for the man to be able to share his feelings and tackle the issues. An opportunity to develop a sense of control of the process is provided, and the man is encouraged to use his existing strengths to aid recovery.

Let's look at the available treatments for working with trauma. Psychological approaches will involve providing support and information. The main focus will be on trauma-focused interventions, which can reduce the symptoms related to the trauma, lessen anxiety and depression, and improve quality of life. They are also effective with people who have experienced prolonged or repeated traumatic events. The main ones are as follows.

Trauma-focused cognitive behaviour therapy

Trauma-focused cognitive behaviour therapy provides information about the effects of trauma, strategies for managing anxiety symptoms, and exposure techniques (see page 73). These techniques help you to deal with the memories of the traumatic experience(s) in a controlled and safe way. Exposure involves gradually recalling and thinking about memories until they no longer create high levels of distress. This may be done through talking or writing.

Trauma-focused cognitive behaviour therapy focuses on your sense of safety in particular, as this is disrupted by traumatic events, leading to hypervigilance, having strong startle reactions and avoiding threatening situations. The therapist may ask you to consider the relevance of safety to you to identify situations in which you feel vulnerable and what it is about those situations (e.g. thoughts, images in your mind) that trigger your trauma, and how you have handled these situations.

You may then be asked to visit a range of related places, recognizing that the traumatic event is unlikely to happen again, that we don't have control over everything that happens to us and that we can't control the behaviour of others. Although the possibility of being exposed to trauma still exists, we can take steps to reduce the possibility of harm to ourselves or others.

It also involves looking at any unhelpful thinking patterns and underlying beliefs related to the trauma. Here is an example:

Another soldier by the name of Steve had been deployed to areas of conflict a number of times. He was struggling with the effects of trauma, and his main concern was the impact of conflict on civilians. He has seen them harmed, and this disturbs him more than anything.

The therapist helped him to understand that he strongly valued justice, and that the effects of the conflict were strongly unjust. His therapy focused on gradual exposure to the memories through writing about them, and also working with his thinking and underlying beliefs. The treatment took time, but Steve responded very well, and the distress subsided.

Eye movement desensitization and reprocessing

Eye movement desensitization and reprocessing combines aspects of cognitive behaviour therapy (exposure) with particular eye movements. The man is asked to recall aspects of the traumatic event while following back-and-forth hand movements by the therapist. This helps the brain process the traumatic experiences. A good analogy is that the memories and emotions related to the trauma, which have been constantly active in the mind, are put away in the 'filing cabinet' of memory in your brain.

Self-care

With recovery from trauma, it is important that men are assisted to manage any related issues, including:

- anxiety or depression (see chapters 3 and 4)
- anger issues (see Chapter 6)
- emotion regulation difficulties (see Chapter 6)
- substance-related issues (see Chapter 5).

It is also important to work on self-care, including establishing routines such as regular sleeping and eating patterns, and exercise. Avoiding self-medicating with substances may be discussed. Staying connected with family and friends and engaging in meaningful activities can also help recovery (see Chapter 2).

Mindfulness may be helpful and is sometimes combined

with cognitive behaviour therapy (see pages 38–39). A sense of hope is encouraged as the various therapies are effective and the symptoms can improve. Consideration during recovery about what has been learnt through the trauma about personal strengths, life, family and coping may assist.

Some centres offer group therapy or residential programs. These tend to be well-received by men who find being able to share what they are going through with other men very helpful. It has been said that to 'to heal, men need other men'.[8] Community-based programs may assist, such as the OneWave 'surf experience', which brings together people who have experienced mental health issues.

TIP: Men benefit from the support of other men. So, seek out group therapy or other programs where you can share your experiences with other men and support each other in recovery.

Remember that relationships can suffer when there has been trauma. For example, a man with post-traumatic stress disorder may be struggling with irritability and feeling dissociated at times. When his children are tired and upset, he might find himself feeling angry or dissociated. His partner may feel upset and frustrated about his response, and conflict may result. Partners or family members may find it helpful to see a doctor or therapist for their own support and assistance, or couples may benefit from relationship counselling (see Chapter 8).

In relation to medication, it is generally not used as a routine first-line treatment in trauma. The trauma-focused psychological approaches are tried first. But it may be used if symptoms are severe, or if the man is not benefitting enough from the therapy alone.

Medication may also be suggested when alternative psychological treatment is not available, or when the person has a co-existing condition, such as significant depression. Often the selective serotonin reuptake inhibitors (SSRIs) are used (see page 88). Medication may also be needed to help with nightmares and sleep.

As the man is treated, how he is feeling and progressing over time needs to be monitored. In particular, doctors and therapists will watch out for thoughts of suicide and self-harm (see Chapter 10).

Narrative therapy

Narrative therapy has been used in Australia to assist Aboriginal people, many of whom have experienced significant trauma. This approach, which sees the individual as the expert on themselves and utilizes stories, sits well with Aboriginal people because stories are an integral part of their culture.[9]

Another group who may need specialized assistance are refugees and asylum seekers who have fled their homeland because of war or persecution. They may have experienced significant trauma through separation from family, death of family members, or experiencing abuse or torture. Specialist organizations can assist.

COPING WITH NATURAL DISASTERS

At times we are affected by natural disasters, such as bushfires or pandemics. We are all familiar with bushfire survival plans, for example, but not so familiar with having a mental health survival plan. It is also important to be psychologically prepared.

At the time around the threat, you need to focus on the warning messages and emergency advice sent out by the experts and follow this advice. During this time be prepared that you may experience stress and anxiety and may need to calm your breathing (take medium–slow breaths), as well as your thoughts. Thoughts that minimize or catastrophize the threat can occur, so take stock of your thinking and focus on helpful realistic thoughts such as, 'We have a plan and we are going to follow it through step by step.' In other words, the three steps involved in being psychologically prepared are:

1. Anticipate that you will feel worried and anxious.
2. Identify the specific feelings and thoughts you are having.
3. Manage them with breathing and calm self-talk.

As the disaster unfolds, humans tend to go into survival mode, doing what needs to be done. Once the threat has passed, you may stay in this mode for some time, and experience a range of physical symptoms, behaviours, thoughts and emotions. Here are some examples:

- Being hyperalert all the time, not sleeping or getting tired/exhausted easily.
- Feeling numb, irritable, anxious, panicky or depressed.
- Feeling disorientated or confused and having visual images of the event or nightmares.
- Withdrawing from others or keeping very busy.

It is important to remember that these responses, even though they can be very distressing, are normal and can last for days or weeks. Here are some tips to help with coping.

TEN TIPS FOR COPING WITH AN EMOTIONAL RESPONSE TO DISASTER

1. Recognize that you have been through a very distressing experience and focus on feeling safe and secure in the first instance.
2. Avoid overusing alcohol or other drugs to cope.
3. Don't bottle up your feelings. Share them with people close to you if you are able to or write them down. If you are a person who expresses yourself through action (e.g. gardening), then do these things.
4. Let key family and friends know about what you need, whether it be practical or emotional support.
5. Maintain a normal routine and do some things you enjoy.
6. Rest when you can and use relaxation techniques (e.g. relaxing each muscle group in the body, breathing effectively — you can download phone apps or borrow CDs from a library to help with this).
7. Eat well and do some exercise.
8. Problem-solve what you need to be doing — seek help with this from family and friends.
9. Be aware that recent trauma may stir up memories from past traumas. Focus on keeping these memories separate in your mind — you can only process so much at one time.
10. Seek professional help if need be.

Trauma can involve a great deal of loss and grief, such as loss of loved ones, property or animals. Recovery from loss and grief takes time and a range of emotions can be experienced. Many of the above tips will be useful and more information on grief can be found in Chapter 6.

Some individuals may have a severe or persistent reaction to stress/trauma and will need to seek help. If you are experiencing significant distress lasting more than a couple of weeks, then please seek help from your doctor who can assess the situation and advise you about appropriate assistance.

Following trauma or a disaster, some men may go on to develop depression or post-traumatic stress disorder. Refer back to Chapter 4 on depression and the earlier section in this chapter on post-traumatic stress disorder and note the resources listed.

WHAT WE HAVE LOOKED AT SO FAR!

A range of traumas can occur at any age and can have far-reaching effects. Trauma may result from event(s) experienced as harmful or possibly life-threatening. The brain is affected by trauma, resulting in higher states of stress and a bigger response to later trauma. It is not weak to be distressed following trauma.

Long-lasting anxiety can occur in post-traumatic stress disorder with ongoing difficulties, such as nightmares or flashbacks, being hypervigilant or more angry or depressed. When the effects of trauma are persistent, and mental health issues become evident, it is important to seek some help from professionals with expertise in the area.

Several therapies can assist (in particular, trauma-focused cognitive therapy and eye movement desensitization and reprocessing). Seeking help from doctors or therapists experienced in this area is key. And at times medication can be very helpful and necessary.

Community-based programs, where men can support other men, can be very valuable. There are also a range of excellent online resources related to trauma and post-traumatic stress disorder.

8.

WORKING ON RELATIONSHIP ISSUES

At the end of the day, you can either focus on what's tearing you apart or what's keeping you together.
Anonymous

Relationships are central to humans, as we all need love and belonging. A healthy partner relationship can bring happiness and be a buffer against adverse events in life; it can be a reservoir of support for both of you to work towards shared goals and take risks in life, such as having or adopting children, or moving countries or creating a home.

We know that men's mental health and wellbeing are impacted positively by relationships, and when there are significant issues in the relationship, there can be negative impacts. Mental health issues can arise out of relationship issues, and key relationships in men's lives can be adversely affected when mental health issues such as anxiety, depression or trauma are present.

There has been a lot of research into the effects on men of being part of a committed relationship. Studies about married men, for example, have shown that they have less physical and mental health problems and they live longer than men who are not married. The responsibilities involved in a committed relationship increase a man's sense of duty, as well as his sense of empowerment.[1]

When a committed relationship ends, there can be significant trauma and despair for the man. Divorce and related issues, such as loss of contact with children or loss of property, can cause great distress.

With over half of couples heading to see a therapist, at least one of them will have already made a decision to separate. They will have a range of reasons for this, but unfortunately a lack of insight into the issues, denial of the problems, or shame can prevent one or both of the individuals from seeking help early enough.

The focus of this chapter will be on prevention. It is mostly about the maintenance of a healthy relationship with the aim of helping you have a fulfilling partner relationship and preventing relationship problems from arising, and thereby protecting your mental health. Some information about what can go significantly wrong in relationships is also provided.

Note that many of the principles covered apply equally to heterosexual and same-sex partner relationships and can be applied to other relationships in life. Let's look at the story of Bob, Jodie and John:

Bob is married to Jodie and they have three adult children who live out of home. Bob and Jodie work full-time, but Bob does not enjoy his work any more and finds it very stressful. His mood has been depressed in recent months.

Bob puts his behaviours down to work stress, but Jodie has been growing more concerned about him. She has noticed that Bob has been increasingly withdrawn and irritable at home. She is also concerned about their relationship, as she 'can't seem to say anything without being growled at'. They have not been sexually intimate for months and she fears they are 'growing apart'. They seek out some assistance.

Their son, John, recently broke up with his girlfriend and moved back in with his parents. He has been struggling with his mood and having a lot of negative thoughts such as, 'What's the point? I'll never have a good relationship,' and drinking more to cope with his feelings of despair. Bob and Jodie have been really worried about him.

WAYS TO MAINTAIN A HEALTHY PARTNER RELATIONSHIP

Humans are social creatures. We live in groups and seek out relationships, including relationships with partners. So, what do we need to know to help these relationships do well over time?

Firstly, there are many myths in the community about relationships, created through generations of fairytales and romantic movies. There may be ideas about finding or being the 'perfect' partner, or that love means an easy path. It is also a myth that each person can be 'everything' to their partner because this is not humanly possible!

Rather than aiming for a fairytale relationship, the aim is to foster a more secure and healthy relationship. The start of a relationship is often a magical time, during which each person sees the best in their partner and is generous and giving. As time goes on, the relationship becomes more real, and individual flaws become more apparent. There can be times with disagreements and conflict. Maintaining the relationship becomes very important and this takes work and effort.

There are a number of strategies to help partner relationships over time, and we are going to look at them now. The strategies relate to connection, communication, caring and compassion, conflict management, creativity and contribution and commitment.

Connection

Humans become 'attached' to other humans; that is, they become linked emotionally and physically. Connection is created through small acts, such as understanding words or a gentle touch, and spending time together. This is why it is important to regularly give full attention to a partner. Here are some useful ways to aid connection:

- Be mindful of each other's values (see pages 22–25). Ask yourself questions such as, 'What sort of personal qualities do I want to bring into my relationship? How do I want to behave or act on an ongoing basis?'
- Work on seeing the world from your partner's point of view. Listen with the aim of understanding and helping the other person feel important (rather than jumping straight into solving the issues).
- Work on letting go of unhelpful stories about the other person or the relationship (e.g. 'I'm not good enough for them,' or 'they/my partner always let me down').

- Be mindful of your partner generally (e.g. become more aware of their facial expressions, body language and speech, or simple things like the foods they like).
- Connect when you leave your partner (e.g. say 'goodbye', 'I love you' or 'have a good day'). Connect as soon as you come back together (e.g. make eye contact, touch, ask how their day was).
- Use 'rituals' to help you connect with your partner, such as a regular date night.

Understanding your partner's emotional language(s) can also help a relationship. Author Gary Chapman talks about 'five love languages', suggesting that individuals express their love for their partner in different ways. These are:

1. words of affirmation
2. quality time
3. receiving gifts
4. acts of service
5. physical touch.[2]

It is not often that a couple have the same love language and they may become confused when their partner does not understand their communication! It is helpful to spend time working out your own and your partner's language(s) and make efforts to develop and use these languages more. To illustrate the value of 'love languages', here is a story about Luke and Sophie:

Luke and Sophie have been together for six months. They are getting to know each other and are both endeavouring to connect more and are both hoping for a long-term relationship. They generally get on well and have similar values; however, at times, they both feel frustrated because they don't seem to be on the same page in expressing how they feel. Sophie enjoys saying how she feels and spending quality time with Luke. She responds to words of affirmation from Luke and time spent together. Luke, however, struggles to find the words to express his feelings. His ways of expressing love are physical touch and acts of service. He often helps Sophie out and is very affectionate physically.

The problem is that these differing love languages seem to cause conflict between Luke and Sophie, when one of them thinks the other is not meeting their needs and feels frustrated or rejected.

You can see how understanding the 'love languages' would help Luke and Sophie. They could then recognize when the other was expressing their love, and they could each work on developing their other love languages.

Therapists John and Julie Gottman speak about the importance of making efforts to 'turn towards' a partner. This means giving a positive response when a partner reaches out for your attention (e.g. they may say 'watch a movie with me' or ask for a hug). In couples close to breaking up, bids for attention are often ignored.

Responding to a bid for attention is critical in helping your partner feel appreciated and connected. It is important to talk about this together and choose some ways you would like each other to 'turn towards' you. Sometimes practical considerations override this, but awareness and talking about it helps prevent feelings of rejection.

Intimacy with a partner involves deep connection. It is about knowing the other person emotionally (their feelings), psychologically (what is on their mind), and physically (touching, sex). Get to know what you and your partner value and want in relation to these areas, and foster connection through validating them with words, gestures (e.g. helping out, giving a gift), and touch (e.g. hugging, kissing, massage).

Communication

Effective communication is essential in relationships. Couples who present for counselling will often say communication has failed. What they are saying is that there are issues such as:

- unclear communication, not listening or not being heard
- a lack of empathy
- dismissing a partner's concerns rather than validating them
- not asking regularly about the other person's wellbeing or life
- not letting the partner know they are cared about
- presuming the partner can 'mind read' your needs, and not actually talking about them
- having expectations that the partner 'should' know about an event or issues, and not communicating about it
- not communicating about difficult topics
- not being able to express needs assertively
- not communicating respectfully
- passive–aggressive patterns of communicating, such as sarcasm or shutting down, or
- verbally abusive communication.

To help communication with a partner, be aware of thinking traps (see page 74) and avoid ones such as 'mind-reading' your partner's thought or generalizing (e.g. you have 'never' understood me). Instead, be more understanding and empathic (step into their shoes), be assertive rather than angry (see page 176), and learn how to express how you feel and ask the other person more often how they feel. Listen carefully and drop any defensiveness. And remember to 'ask nicely' when communicating your needs. We teach children to do this, but sometimes we forget as adults. It is an antidote to asking in a passive–aggressive way (e.g. 'If you can be bothered, can you clean up the kitchen?') or an angry way.[3] Following are some tips for improving communication.

NINE SKILLS FOR IMPROVING COMMUNICATION

1. Don't criticize.
2. Don't become defensive.
3. Don't use contempt.
4. Don't stonewall (shut out the other person).
5. Do calm down.
6. Do be assertive.
7. Do speak non-defensively.
8. Do validate by listening.
9. Do overlearn these skills![4]

Caring and compassion

Any relationship requires caring and kindness and being a good friend to the other person. When each person is appreciated, they are more likely to be kind to the other. To increase your appreciation:

- Notice three things you appreciate about your partner.
- Contemplate what your partner adds to your life.
- Reflect on your partner's strengths.
- Say 'thank you' more often and let them know what you are grateful for in relation to them!

Caring and compassion require empathy and acknowledging that your partner is sometimes in pain. It is important to look at situations from your partner's perspective and ask, 'What (are they) afraid of? Why does this matter to (them)?'[5] And don't forget to be kind to yourself as well. Practise greater self-care and drop self-critical thoughts.

Compromise

Couples need to tolerate the faults of their partner and be able to compromise or make concessions and find the middle ground. Research about willingness to compromise highlights that:

- Compromise involves being able to consider the other person's position, accepting the other person's influence and finding some common ground.
- Accepting the other person's influence encourages respect, learning, compromise, positivity and a strong friendship.
- When compromise is needed, aim to soften discussion and be calm and respectful.

CHOOSE A PROBLEM NEEDING SOME COMPROMISE

Each person needs to sit separately, reflect on the problem and answer these questions:

- What do we agree about?
- What are our common feelings or the most important feelings here?
- What common goals can we have here?
- How can we understand this situation or issue?
- How do we think these goals should be achieved?

Now come together as a couple and talk through your answers.

Another useful tool when there is a hard situation to resolve and compromise is necessary comes from acceptance and commitment therapy. Called the LOVE formula, it suggests:

- Letting go of resentment, blaming, judging, criticizing and being demanding.
- Opening up to the painful feelings related to the relationship, and to the partner's feelings, acknowledging feelings are important.
- Valuing by caring, contributing and connection; connecting with values can assist by focusing on what is important and not sweating the small things.
- Engaging or being psychologically present and able to focus on the partner.[6]

Conflict management

Couples who go to counselling often report problems with conflict in the relationship. Some of the common topics discussed by couples are time spent together and apart, money, health, and gender differences (in heterosexual relationships) which influence the relationship. The most common causes of conflict are finances, housework, the first child, in-laws and sex.

Research about heterosexual relationships has shown that for women, discontent often stems from the perception that their partner does not listen when they make an effort to communicate or are unable to meet their emotional needs. The studies conclude that men are sensitive to their partners' complaints but may struggle to know what to do about them. They may focus on what to do to fix the problem, which may be appropriate, but the partner may want to first focus on how they feel about the problem, and this can trigger conflict.

These differences arise from disparities in brain function. Men process emotions and words differently in the brain compared to women. This does not mean that one gender is right or superior, it's just that there are differences in strengths. Mutual respect is important; men being told they are not competent in an aspect of a relationship often increases feelings of helplessness or anxiety.[7]

Interestingly, research indicates that many partner arguments cannot be fully 'resolved'. This is because there may be different views based on previous life experiences (e.g. the type of school a child should go to, or where to invest money). Acceptance of this is important as well as working on a compromise together. Here are some helpful tips for dealing with conflict in relationships.

STRATEGIES FOR DEALING WITH CONFLICT

- Be aware of unhelpful thinking patterns which may come into play as conflict escalates (see page 107). Watch out for unrealistic expectations of the other person.

- Understand that you have the most control over your behaviours, rather than your thoughts or feelings. Focus on helpful behaviours, such as listening, and reduce unhelpful ones, such as criticizing.

- When conflict is escalating, take time out from the discussion. Couples need to talk about this together ahead of time, as sometimes in arguments one person will 'run' (or move away) and the other person will 'chase' them. Consider how each of you feel in this instance (e.g. anxious, abandoned) and work out a plan to allow each of you to have some time out if need be.

- When there are difficult emotions, such as anxiety or hurt, individuals need to be able to soothe themselves, and then each other. Self-soothing may take 20 minutes or so. Let your partner know that you are feeling overwhelmed and need some time out, then do something you know helps you feel calmer, such as exercise or meditation. Once you are both calm, you are then able to soothe each other.

- Let go of the need to have the last word, or take off your 'armour' and put down your sword! This means that you need to allow yourself to be vulnerable and open yourself up to some painful feelings.

- Be aware of the stories you or your partner have developed which feed conflict (see page 115). One might be the 'it is not safe to trust' story, in which the person is hyper-alert for signs of betrayal because of past experiences; and another is the 'housework' story, about who is contributing more or less. These stories can lead to repetitive or 'pet' arguments, and

they need to be acknowledged and worked through with understanding. You might want to agree to leave some of these 'pet' arguments outside![8]
- Take responsibility for conflict at times. Ask yourself questions like, 'What did I say or do to worsen things? Can I admit some role in creating the conflict? What are some more helpful actions?'

Importantly, couples often argue about topics that are associated with control and power. One or each person may be determined to have their own way, but if we expect everyone else to see things the way we do, then we are more likely to try to exert power and control over others. This often leads to more and more conflict, and a negative effect on the relationship over time. More flexibility is needed.

There has been a lot written about the need for 'fair fighting'. Too often, individuals use 'dirty fighting' tactics rather than 'fair fighting'. Dirty fighting refers to tactics used to win an argument or inflict pain. Author Russ Harris highlights issues with 'dirty fighting' including:

- Going off-topic and unleashing something the person did wrong in the past.
- Ganging up by getting a third party involved in the argument.
- Being mean and focusing on something you know will upset the other person.
- Twisting the other person's words, taking them out of context or exaggerating them.
- Throwing objects or slamming doors (we will look at domestic violence in a moment).[9]

Part of managing these tactics is having some rules about 'fair fighting'. These rules can help you deal with conflict more effectively and save relationships from breaking down. They include:

- Beforehand, ask yourself why you feel upset. Discuss one issue at a time and stay with the topic.
- Do not use degrading language.
- Express feelings in words and take responsibility for them, for example, 'I feel angry and hurt.'
- Avoid stonewalling or shutting the other person out.
- Avoid yelling.
- Take time out if need be.
- Attempt to come to a compromise.

FAIR FIGHTING

With your partner, brainstorm the dirty fighting tactics you have used in the past. Maintain a sense of humour while you do this! Then lay out your new fair fighting rules.

The Gottmans also stress the importance of making 'repair attempts' in relationships. These involve words or actions aimed at repairing the relationship after conflict. Practice is often needed to recognize attempts at repair. Focusing on the words being used can help, for example, sentences beginning with 'I feel

…' or 'I appreciate …' may be a repair attempt, or statements such as, 'I need to calm down', 'Can we take a rest' or 'Sorry'.

Conflict can also be about resentment. Resentment can build up over time and it can eat away at positive feelings. Examples of issues which might cause resentment include one person perceiving that they are left to do all the housework or child-rearing, or another person believing that they sacrificed their career for the other person. Forgiveness can offer relief from resentment. It means pardoning the person and letting go of resentments. It is not easy, but it is powerful. Remember that forgiveness does not involve forgetting or excusing, but it does involve LOVE: Letting go, Opening up, Valuing and Engaging.

Creativity

Creativity refers to seeing the world in a different way, tapping into your inner strengths and developing new ideas. You can apply creativity to relationships and help them flourish! Creativity can be used when dealing with problems through being creative about problem-solving (see pages 69–71). Think laterally when coming up with possible solutions to problems.

It can be also used to instill some fun and flexibility into relationships, and to revive intimacy. Creativity can be applied to appreciating each other and finding new ways to express this and applying the 'five love languages'. A good starting point involves creating shared meaning in relationships. This might involve:

- Revisiting your values.
- Exploring your relationship, that is, how you do things and if there are particular rituals (e.g. how birthdays are celebrated).

- Looking at how you and your partner support each other's dreams.
- Exploring any spiritual dimensions to the relationship.
- Sharing the stories of each person in the relationship.
- Remembering that romance can be woven into rituals to foster intimacy (e.g. a regular 'date night' at home, sharing a bath or massage as part of the evening).

Here is a story of a couple who saw a therapist for couple counselling. They found some creative ways to get their relationship back on track:

> Joe and Mary, a professional couple in their mid-thirties with two young children, were finding that they were arguing more and more and not spending much quality time together. They felt distant from each other. They explored their relationship and shared values with a therapist and talked about their shared stories and goals. The therapist suggested they reconnect with each other by finding more time to be together. They were asked to think about this creatively.
>
> Joe and Mary decided to have regular 'date nights' out and at home. They organized babysitting each fortnight and guarded this time together. Gradually they felt more connected and more content in their relationship.

Now think about some ways you might be more creative in your relationship. Here is an exercise to assist.

Contribution and commitment

Healthy relationships require both contribution and commitment by partners. Here are some tools from the Gottmans to build on your contribution and commitment:

- Consider how committed you are to the relationship. Use a scale of 0 to 10, where 0 is no commitment and 10 is the most committed you could be. What did you find? Are you surprised? Do you need to work on this?
- With your partner consider how you see your different roles in the relationship. These will influence the contributions made. Discuss and explore the possibilities.
- Be mindful of unhelpful thinking about expectations of each other. Watch out for any underlying beliefs, such as 'being taken for granted', which may push your thinking around.

- Talk through your various life goals together.
- With specific areas such as finances, discuss concerns and work on managing any issues together (see pages 69–71).
- Connect with each other and learn to soothe one another when one is stressed.

MAINTAINING CONTRIBUTION AND COMMITMENT IN FIVE 'MAGIC' HOURS PER WEEK

1. With partings, ensure that before saying goodbye in the morning you've learnt one thing happening in your partner's life that day (2 minutes a day × 5 working days = 10 minutes per week).
2. On reunion, discuss any stressful events from the day (20 minutes a day × 5 working days = 1 hour 40 minutes).
3. Show daily admiration and appreciation for your partner (5 minutes a day × 7 days = 35 minutes).
4. Show affection each day, for example, kiss your partner before sleep (5 minutes a day × 7 days = 35 minutes).
5. Have a weekly date and turn towards each other (2 hours × 1 day = 2 hours).[10]

Commitment may involve going to couple counselling for a period of time or intermittently if you need to work on this in your relationship.

FOSTERING A HEALTHY SEXUAL RELATIONSHIP

When we think about a healthy relationship, we tend to think the sexual side has to be good. This part of a relationship is critical to its health. Research has shown that it is actually the affection that accompanies sex that is most important, and that everyday kissing, hugging and touch is key to a relationship.[11] Some people struggle to show affection (remember the love languages), and sometimes expectations may need to be reduced and they may need to practise affection to learn to be more comfortable with it.

TIP: Foster everyday affection in your partner relationship. Affection is also the key to a healthy sexual relationship.

Sex also produces a natural elevation of mood or a 'high' due to changes in the brain. But more importantly, sex creates connection between partners because they feel more attached.

Sexual disconnection, on the other hand, is a common cause of dissatisfaction and distress in relationships and is often talked about in couple therapy. There may be dissatisfaction about differing sex drives and frequency of sexual relations, or about specific sexual issues. As we look at these, remember that most sexual health issues benefit from attention to the relationship generally, as well as to specific sexual issues. Here are some points in relation to sex drive:

- In terms of dissatisfaction about frequency, men have higher testosterone levels which leads to a difference in sex drive.
- Interestingly, men who do more housework report more frequent sex, and women who feel loved and cared for have improved sexual functioning.[12]
- Taking into account factors such as health and stage in life is important. Chronic health issues and some

medications may limit sex drive (for example, some medication for high blood pressure or antidepressants).

- Going through a busy stage in life with young children or in relation to work may also be an issue. Overwork or being overly busy in life can get in the way, as can stress and anxiety. So have a good look at you and your partner's lifestyles and priorities and consider adjusting them if need be.

- A common theme in dealing with differing sex drives is to make sure to nurture your relationship generally. Working on your sense of connection and intimacy is key (e.g. spending more time together talking or dating, adding more light touch or massage into the relationship).

Now we are going to focus on issues with sexual functioning, which means that normal sexual responding is disrupted or not adequate. There may be a problem with erection (an inability to get or to maintain an erection), or problems with ejaculation or orgasm. These issues may be long-term or have occurred more recently, and one problem may be triggering another.

The causes of sexual dysfunction will vary, but will be related to physical or psychological functioning, or the relationship. Age is a significant factor in relation to erection, with men over 50 years of age being more likely to report problems. Surgery for prostate problems may cause erectile dysfunction, along with a number of health conditions such as obesity, diabetes or high blood pressure, or various conditions of the nervous system.

There will be an overlap between physical, psychological and relationship factors. For example, a distressing relationship may impact the man's psychological wellbeing, which in turn influences his physical sexual response. Or there may be a medical reason for difficulties with erection, which then impacts intimacy and the relationship. A sexual issue may be caused by one factor, but then maintained by another, so it is vital to consider any psychological factors related to sexual issues.

For example, loss of erection due to stress or medication may reduce self-confidence and trigger anxiety about functioning sexually, which then perpetuates the problem. It may be that a man is self-critical and anxious about his sexual response and this may erode his self-confidence. He may overly monitor his own sexual response, taking the focus off the moment, or he may tend to measure up to unrealistic stereotypes and expectations (fostered by society and media) and have a sense of not meeting them.

Depression and anxiety may cause problems with sexual functioning as well, but also result from them. Past trauma can also impact. Take some time to refer back to these issues in chapters 3, 4 and 7. In terms of treatment, it is important to look at the health of the relationship and anything that may be interfering with intimacy, communication and commitment in the relationship.

In terms of 'performance anxiety', let go of the thought that sex has to be a performance. It is about intimacy and enjoyment. Lessen the need to self-monitor, and stop self-critical evaluation. Relax your body and be mindful and focus on all the pleasurable sensations. Hypnotherapy may assist in lessening this form of anxiety.

It is also important to look at general health, including quitting smoking, losing weight, reducing stress and exercising. Many men are reluctant to do this because they feel embarrassed about their sexual issues. But there is help available and it is good to start with a check-up with your doctor and looking at any physical factors which may be contributing. They will do a general check including some blood tests. They can assist with referrals to a counsellor or sex therapist and advise on whether medication might be helpful.

THINGS THAT CAN GO VERY WRONG IN A RELATIONSHIP

Life is all about relationships but sometimes things can go wrong within them. We do not have the space here to look at all the problems that can arise, but we will consider a few of them. The key advice is to recognize them and deal with them early. This may involve just you, or you and your family, or seeking help from professionals. You may need to call on a doctor, mental health professional, couple therapist or lawyer.

....

TIP: If you think things are going wrong in a relationship, seek help *early*.

....

We will look at a few important relationship problems, namely infidelity, domestic violence, separation and divorce.

Infidelity

Let's talk about infidelity in general as your partner may have had an affair, or you may have had one. An affair refers to an intense emotional or sexual relationship (sex or inappropriate physical contact) with someone other than your partner.[13] Dealing with infidelity is very difficult for a couple. It is a painful process due to the distress caused and can have a very destructive effect on the relationship.

Social media has led to a new type of affair. What may start out as a flirtation can lead to a significant 'emotional affair' and an addiction to the thrill of online involvement with someone. Emotional affairs are more common than sexual affairs. Research has found that women are more upset about emotional affairs, and men are more concerned about sexual affairs.

There are a number of potential causes of infidelity. It may be that monogamy is a struggle for an individual. We know that people who are unfaithful in one relationship are more likely to be unfaithful in their next one, compared to those who have not been unfaithful in the first one. There may be a lack of emotional connection between partners, or possibly emotional dissatisfaction in the relationship. And if aspects of the relationship are triggering low self-worth, this may contribute. There may also be underlying problems stemming from past trauma or sexual addictions.

DEALING WITH INFIDELITY TO SAVE A RELATIONSHIP

- Acknowledge what has happened between you and your partner.
- If the affair involved a sexual relationship, have a check for sexually transmitted infections.
- Talk about the infidelity together.
- Know that you can only be responsible for your own fidelity.
- Agree that the affair must end.
- Seek out couple therapy to explore what happened, the associated feelings and any underlying issues in the relationship.

An affair involves a very significant breach of trust. It needs to be rebuilt and this takes time. The partner who has broken the trust must be willing to explore their actions to see what has contributed, and the couple needs to look at the relationship and any problem areas.

Trust must be earned again via actions, including speaking honestly and being reliable. Sometimes amends may need to be made by validating the other person's feelings, expressing remorse, apologizing for the hurt, showing more appreciation for the other person and spending time together.

In developing trust, focus on trusting in small ways first, then gradually larger actions of trust can be taken. If you don't feel safe with your partner, trust your intuition. If your partner is not getting some help, it is hard to trust things are getting better.

Acceptance is also needed: that you may never be certain that your partner will not repeat the behaviours but they are committed and making an effort.

There are a couple of other points to be aware of in relation to infidelity. At times, an individual will see a therapist because they are feeling guilty about the affair. They want to tell the other person to ease their own distress. However, this should not be the main motivation for telling a partner. You need to put your partner's needs ahead of your own in this situation and then make a decision.

Also, the result of an affair may be that a couple make a decision to have a more open relationship. This involves being committed to the relationship but having sex outside the relationship and being honest about this. Some people can manage this, but many others can't. Those individuals with a more anxious attachment style (see later in this chapter) will struggle with this, and anxiety and jealousy can arise.

Domestic violence

Domestic violence can occur no matter what your age, gender or sexual orientation. Although rates of violence against women are higher in the community, domestic violence may be perpetrated by men or women.

The term 'domestic violence' refers to 'violence, abuse and intimidation between people who are currently or have previously been in an intimate relationship'. Violence is used to control and dominate the other person, and this causes fear and potentially physical or psychological harm. Domestic violence is a violation of human rights.[14]

Some communities, such as Aboriginal and Torres Strait Islander communities, prefer the term 'family violence'. Family violence refers to violence between family members (for example, children and parents), as well as intimate partners. Here are a few important points about domestic violence:

- It can include physical assault, sexual assault, verbal abuse, emotional abuse, financial abuse, technology-facilitated abuse, social abuse (isolating someone from their supports) or spiritual abuse (stopping someone from practising their religion).
- At the centre of abuse is a controlling behaviour pattern. It may include going through a partner's text messages, emails and social media, controlling money, criticizing continuously, ignoring the person or refusing to talk, or emotional blackmail, for example, 'If you loved me, you would ...' In a relationship, threats to hurt, kill or rape can be about control.
- There is often a cycle of violence; that is, there is a tension-building phase with conflict and abuse, followed by a peak of violence (an 'explosion').

A honeymoon phase follows with remorse and promises of no more violence. There can be denial of the problem during this phase. The cycle repeats itself over time.

In addition, when a partner has significant personality issues, such as narcissistic personality traits or disorder, they may be more likely to perpetrate abusive behaviours. Those with narcissistic personality features often have an exaggerated sense of their own importance, but lack empathy and often have issues in relationships at work or at home. Underneath it all, their self-esteem is very fragile.

For these reasons controlling a partner serves to help the person feel more powerful. Some behaviours are very characteristic of narcissistic abuse, such as blaming the other person or isolating them from loved ones, stonewalling (withdrawing completely) or gaslighting (making you distrust your perceptions about reality or your mental wellbeing).

Men need to be alert to being abused, or to perpetrating abuse, and seek help. Most countries will have government websites and services (such as national phone hotlines) addressing domestic violence. Some therapists specialize in this area or there may be group programs available. Social workers may be able to assist a person leaving an abusive relationship (see also the Resources section at the end of the book).

TIP: If there is an emergency in relation to domestic violence CALL the emergency services number in your location.

Separation and divorce

Unfortunately, it is common that many men do not see separation and divorce coming. They can be blindsided and thrown into shock and devastation as a result. However, research tells us there are some signs that a long-term relationship will eventually end, including:

- There is a readiness for conflict.
- There have been failed repair attempts (or attempts to mend a relationship after conflict), in combination with criticism, defensiveness, contempt and shutting down.
- One or both partners rewrite or change the relationship stories about the past (e.g. 'We should never have gotten together, we weren't suited', 'My partner has never liked intimacy …').
- The couple is leading parallel lives or feel lonely.

TIP: If you are experiencing overwhelming emotions after separation or divorce, or are having suicidal thoughts, seek help from your doctor or emergency services.

Men report having a number of intense experiences around the time of separation and divorce, from shock and hurt, to anger, relief, desperation or sadness. There can be a rollercoaster of emotions. Multiple losses can be involved, including family, friends, home and home routines, contact with children, dreams for the future and finances.

Attachments are disrupted when a relationship ends and significant distress, grief, anxiety or depression can occur. A man's sense of identity can be severely challenged, and men are more at risk of suicide after a relationship breakdown.

Men may use various ways to cope, including suppressing feelings, denial of the situation or substance use. They may use activities that normally help them deal with emotions, such as throwing themselves into work or exercise, or they may seek out support from family and friends.

Studies carried out in the USA found that women initiate most divorces and that men speak about being the discarded partner and often remain attached to their ex-wives. Most men do not remain in the marital home and tend to re-partner more quickly than women.[15]

Adapting to the losses and working through the grief of divorce takes time and it can be a bumpy ride (see Chapter 6). The practical issues, such as financial settlements and child custody issues, may also take significant time. However, men often exhibit remarkable resiliency, assess their losses and what they have learnt and are able to adapt and move forward in life.

Men needing assistance may benefit from support from a therapist. Crisis intervention may be necessary, attending to any signs of depression or anxiety, and suicide risk. Addressing any unhelpful thinking is important initially, as is having the chance to work through emotions. Later therapy can assist with tasks and problem-solving related to separation and divorce.

TIPS FROM MEN WHO HAVE BEEN THROUGH SEPARATION AND DIVORCE

- Be clear that the separation and the relationship may not be able to be 'fixed' quickly.
- Be honest with yourself and take responsibility for your life.
- Be clear about where you have choices and where you don't.

- Listen to your self-talk. Watch out for signs of hopelessness.
- Avoid blame whenever possible.
- Think about the consequences of what you decide to do.
- Talk to people about how things are for you.
- Continue with normal activities and routines.
- Look after yourself and practise self-care (keep eating, exercising and sleeping).

And remember to seek out expert advice and support from a doctor, mental health professional or lawyer when needed. Remember that knowing your legal rights is important.

UNDERSTANDING PATTERNS OF ATTACHMENT

What we know is that relationships are all about 'attachments' to others. Attachment refers to a long-lasting emotional bond with a specific person, whom we actively want to be close to. There is a theory on this called 'attachment theory'. Early attachments are with parents or caregivers and shape our expectations and behaviours in later relationships.

When parents or caregivers are responsive to their infant's needs, this provides what is called a 'safe base' for the infant to then explore their world. Developing a secure attachment helps men learn to manage their emotions and helps them in later partner relationships. Based on some studies of infants and their parents or caregivers, several main patterns or styles of attachment have been identified:

- **Secure style:** The infant learnt that the parent was a safe base, responded to their needs and helped regulate their emotions. If an adult has a secure attachment style, they feel okay with displaying interest and affection, as well as with being alone and independent. They can cope with rejection and are less prone to obsessing over their relationships. They report being happiest in relationships, and they tend to choose partners well, because they are not interested in being treated badly by others.

- **Insecure avoidant style:** The infant experienced a lack of intimacy with the parent and there was less tolerance of the infant being upset. The infant learnt that the parent did not respond to their emotions, especially when they were needy or angry, so they learnt to repress their feelings and become independent. Adults with avoidant attachment are often uncomfortable with intimacy. They may avoid commitment or construct their lifestyle to avoid too much contact with their partners (e.g. by working away or keeping a full schedule). Men with avoidant attachment often partner with those with an anxious style (see next point), as they provide validation for each other. Those with a more avoidant style need to foster their ability to be intimate emotionally with a partner and not pull away, and to allow mutual support.

- **Insecure ambivalent (or anxious) style:** The infant with this style learnt that even if the parent was physically present, they would sometimes but not necessarily always soothe them. As result they tend to 'overactivate' their attachment system and become clingy. Adult men with an anxious attachment style have difficulty in being single compared with the other styles and, as a result, are more likely to have unhealthy relationships. They need plenty of reassurance from their partners, and trust issues may occur. If they partner with someone with an avoidant style, there will be challenges. However, if those with an anxious style learn to communicate their needs and choose secure partners, then more fulfilling relationships can result.

- **Disorganized or chaotic style:** These infants often experienced physical or sexual abuse, and the parents may have had severe mental health or substance-related issues. The infant learnt to be fearful of the parent, as the parent also represented danger. They displayed a chaotic mix of behaviours (moving towards the parent, then away). Adults with this style of attachment tend to have chaotic relationships, with conflict and many crises.[16, 17]

This model can help you understand how you respond in relationships. It is said that psychological issues occur and interpersonal relationships break down when an individual's need for attachment is not being met. This can occur both when the man cannot effectively communicate his needs and when the other person is not able to respond adequately to his needs. Importantly, being aware of you and your partner's styles can help you understand behaviours, be less distressed by them, and work on changing them.

WHAT WE HAVE LOOKED AT SO FAR!

Life is all about connecting with others. Relationships can bring great joy, but also great distress. To maintain healthy partner relationships and therefore assist your mental health and wellbeing, focus on these areas: connection, communication, caring and compassion, compromise, conflict management, creativity, and contribution and commitment.

Effort is required in relationships, and there are many helpful tools to assist you. It is important to practise 'fair fighting' and to make genuine efforts to repair the relationship after conflict.

Sex is an important part of the relationship. It is about affection, connection and enjoyment. Sexual functioning can be impacted by a range of issues, including the health of the relationship. Help is available to address the physical and psychological causes of sexual dysfunction.

Remember Bob and Jodie, and their son John? Let's take a moment to catch up with them:

Bob went to see his doctor about feeling stressed and low, and Jodie went as well to share her concerns. The doctor said that he thought Bob was struggling with depressed mood and he was referred to therapy. Bob also decided to take some time off work and began to exercise again.

Bob and Jodie gradually reconnected by spending more time together. They made the decision to reduce their work hours, so they could continue to do more things together. Bob's sexual drive returned slowly over time, but he was still having problems with maintaining an erection. The doctor did some checks and suggested using some medication.

After a big weekend of drinking, John turned up at a friend's house and they suggested he see a counsellor to help with his mood and dark thoughts. The break-up had hit him very hard, and he was relieved to get some support and help. Bob and Jodie were also relieved he was seeking help, and John gradually worked through the loss of the relationship and got back on track.

You can see how Bob and John reached out for some help and their situation improved. The key is to seek help early when relationship problems emerge. There are many approaches and tools that can assist. Remember too that how individuals behave in a relationship can reflect their earlier attachments, and therapy around this can be very useful.

Domestic violence issues need to be urgently addressed, whether it is taking responsibility for abusive behaviours or seeking help in relation to a partner's behaviours. Separation and divorce can be very distressing and it takes time to work through the associated loss and grief, and to re-establish your identity and life.

To finish the chapter, Alex has reflected on relationships. Here are his thoughts from the chapter about the main tips for a healthy relationship.

TEN TIPS FOR HEALTHY RELATIONSHIPS

1. Connect regularly and listen to each other.
2. Appreciate each other and the small things.
3. Communicate about your feelings.
4. Keep intimacy alive.
5. Get to know the person well.
6. Manage conflict in healthy ways.
7. Have shared goals and respect each other's dreams.
8. Be creative in relationships (e.g. try new things together).
9. Make time for date nights.
10. Be committed to the relationship and put in the effort.

9.

COMMON DISORDERS THAT AFFECT MEN'S MENTAL HEALTH

Together we can face any challenges as deep as the ocean and as high as the sky.

Sonia Gandhi

The field of mental health is very broad, so it is not possible to cover all of the disorders that can affect men's mental health in this book. However, in this chapter we will explore the following mental health issues:

- autism and attention disorders
- eating disorders and body dysmorphia
- psychosis
- dementia.

These disorders are not necessarily related, and they may appear at different stages in life. For example, autism and attention disorders may be diagnosed in early childhood, whereas eating disorders, body dysmorphia and psychosis may become apparent in the teens or early adulthood, and dementia usually occurs in older men. We suggest you read the section(s) relevant to you and check out the resources at the end of the book. Some information about each issue is provided with a focus on possible treatments.

AUTISM

Here is Anthony's story:

> Anthony, a 28-year-old factory worker, saw his doctor and then a therapist as his parents were concerned about him. He had done well at school and university but could not get a job in his field and so he took a factory job, which he liked.
>
> Upon seeing a therapist, Anthony said that he had made few friends and his main social outings were going swimming and visiting his parents. Anthony was not in a relationship and had not had a significant relationship as yet.
>
> The therapist, who was experienced in the field of autism, thought Anthony may have mild features of autism. Anthony worked with the therapist on his social and job interviewing skills and decided to join a swimming club to meet some new people.

Autism is part of what is called 'neurodiversity' in humans. This means there are variations between people in the development of their nervous system, including the brain. With autism, in fact, there can be a very wide range of variations (from mild symptoms to those which are very severe and disabling), and this is often spoken of as an autism 'spectrum'.

Autism often becomes evident in the early years of life, and it persists into adulthood. There are various theories about why it occurs, including our genetics, parents being older in age, and environmental factors (such as viruses) triggering a tendency to autism.[1] Autism is characterized by:

- Difficulties in communication (language, social and non-verbal cues).
- Repetitive patterns of behaviour or interests, such as repeatedly feeling a texture or being focused on numbers. It is thought that these patterns of behaviours may occur to distract the person from distressing symptoms, such as anxiety.
- Sensory issues, so that people with autism may be intolerant of various stimuli touching the skin (e.g. certain clothing), or they may struggle to eat a range of foods. Rocking behaviours or making sounds may block out other sensory input being experienced as disturbing.

Individuals with autism have a greater prevalence of mental health issues such as anxiety, mood, attention and psychotic disorders. Issues with anxiety are extremely common in people with autism. This can play a significant part in triggering issues with behaviours.

A thorough assessment is needed to identify autism. This includes looking at family history, recurrent behaviours such as those already mentioned, and assessing a person's communication and cognitive abilities. Medical assessments such as a physical examination and hearing and vision tests also need to be done.

TIP: It is important to have an assessment by experienced professionals to confirm that autism is present. Contact your doctor, local children's hospital or regional autism organization for assistance to find appropriately trained professionals.

A range of treatment and therapy options are available. These include:

- education about autism
- behavioural therapy
- occupational therapy (including sensory training)
- music therapy
- speech therapy
- social skills training
- life skills coaching
- communication skills training
- psychological therapies for anxiety and depression
- education and learning supports
- support groups (e.g. for teenagers with autism)
- psychiatry and medications, if needed
- supports for family and carers.[2]

ATTENTION DISORDERS

When you think of attention disorders, such as attention deficit hyperactivity disorder (ADHD), you may visualize very active and noisy boys who don't sit still but, in reality, these disorders affect both sexes and all age groups and hyperactivity may or may not be an issue. In attention disorders there can be difficulties with:

- getting started on tasks
- keeping attention on the task at hand and avoiding distraction
- remembering to do things or losing things
- being impulsive (acting without thinking things through)
- planning and organizing

- being on time
- managing emotions, such as frustration and boredom.

These difficulties are thought to be related to lowered levels of the chemical messenger dopamine in particular parts of the brain. Dopamine helps us give attention to tasks.

By adulthood, some of these behaviours may be less of a problem, may occur in different ways, or other difficulties may become more apparent. Some men will continue to struggle with maintaining attention and have difficulties with absorbing and remembering instructions, for example. They may be easily distracted by noise or have difficulty prioritizing, organizing or finishing tasks at work. They may also struggle with motivation or time management.

Other men may have issues with hyperactive behaviours, such as being restless, talking constantly, rushing through activities, or have difficulty shutting off the mind at night. Some will experience impulsive behaviours, including undertaking an activity without thinking through the consequences or blurting out comments without seeming to realize their impact.

KEY POINT

Men with attention disorders may have difficulty tolerating boredom and seek out stimulating activities. These may include addictive behaviours such as overeating or substance use, or they may undertake high-risk behaviours.

Difficulties regulating emotions may also occur, resulting in feeling overwhelmed, having angry outbursts, feeling socially anxious or developing low self-worth. All of these challenges can result in the man struggling with education or achieving life goals, and possibly working long hours due to inefficiency or having performance issues at work.

There may also be difficulties maintaining relationships or financial difficulties due to impulsive spending. There can be legal consequences secondary to impulsive behaviours, and this is more likely if there are associated substance use issues.

It is vital to have a thorough assessment by professionals experienced in assessing attention issues. Diagnosis is based on the symptoms and the length of time they have been present. There are many treatment options available, including:

- education about the attention issues
- working on lifestyle factors (e.g. regular sleep, exercise and healthy foods)
- assistance with issues, such as sleep problems
- supplements such as omega-3 oils
- psychological therapies including cognitive behaviour therapy, relaxation training and mindfulness
- skills training (e.g. regulating attention, communication skills, time management and emotional regulation to manage frustration or anger)
- building self-confidence
- dealing with any risk-taking behaviours, addictions and substance-related issues
- support groups
- possibly medication (stimulant drugs are used to increase dopamine levels).

Authors Greg Crosby and Tonya Lippert discuss an interesting idea. They say that the problem with attention disorders is actually regulating attention, rather than a lack of attention. This means that some men struggle to focus on more mundane activities (due to problems with dopamine levels) and are biased towards very interesting or stimulating activities (which give instant gratification and trigger more dopamine). They suggest learning skills to regulate action and attention (see also the Resources section at the end of the book). These include:

- Modifying your environment to keep you on track. This might involve minimizing distractions (e.g. turning off the television or social media and having reminders about what you are working towards, such as signs, pictures, planners or using timers or alarms for activities. You can make use of your mobile phone to give you reminders).
- Using a planner to write down what you need to do or need to remember. Breaking tasks down into chunks and setting a time to stop (maybe set an alarm) may help.
- Aiming to arrive early instead of on time, if you are always late.
- Reviewing your planner and current obligations before you commit to something. Checking you have time for more commitments and saying 'no' if you don't.
- Giving yourself a reward when you regulate your attention and action (such as spending a certain amount of time doing an activity you enjoy).
- Using more mindfulness in conversation and activities.

Earlier we looked at a strategy called 'surf an urge' (see page 67). Urges to act are like waves; they come and go. Sometimes we obey them at the start, rather than letting them come and go. Here are some reminders about surfing an urge, with ideas particularly related to attention issues. Think about a social situation and struggling with an urge to interrupt a conversation and apply the following ideas.

URGE SURFING WHEN ATTENTION IS A PROBLEM!

- Prepare for different social situations by being mindful and focusing on your breathing beforehand.
- When in the situation, notice an urge without judging or fighting it.
- Notice how it affects your body and any sensations you may be having.
- Notice any thoughts and see whether they need to be shared as urgently as you feel.
- Breathe and let the urge come and go.

You can also use STOP!

Stop.

Take a breath.

Observe — where is your attention?

Proceed — if your attention is distracted, return to where it needs to be.[3]

EATING DISORDERS

Eating disorders have become a major health problem in Australia and across the world. There are a growing number of men with eating disorders. In June 2019, the Butterfly Foundation reported that 360,000 Australian men were living with an eating disorder, and these numbers are likely to increase. Other western countries are also experiencing high rates as well.

Eating disorders are psychological and medical disorders that involve serious abnormalities in eating and weight control behaviours. Unfortunately, they can become chronic and some individuals will die due to the eating disorder. The most common eating disorders are anorexia nervosa, which is a refusal to maintain a minimally normal body weight, and bulimia nervosa, which is repeated episodes of binge eating followed by inappropriate compensatory behaviours such as self-induced vomiting, misuse of laxatives, diuretics or other medications, fasting or excessive exercise. A disturbance in the perception of body shape and weight is an essential feature of both anorexia and bulimia.

Eating disorders are thought to result from biological, psychological and social factors, including genetic vulnerability, stage of development (more at risk in adolescence), personality style (e.g. being perfectionistic), relationship and family problems, and the influences of society and culture.

The child or young man with an eating disorder may be taken in to see a doctor because of concerns about their eating or weight, or issues with body image. Or they may attend with vague symptoms such as tiredness or constipation. Remember that those experiencing eating disorders can have a normal weight.

Despite the seriousness of many of the symptoms of eating disorders, there may be denial that there is a problem. Anxiety (social anxiety, obsessive and compulsive symptoms) and depression can occur with eating disorders. The person may withdraw from family and friends. There may be difficulties sleeping or concentrating at school or work. Self-confidence will be affected. Self-harm and suicidal thinking may occur. Here is Phil's story:

> Phil, a 20-year-old university student, had had a stressful year. His mother had been seriously unwell, he was working 20 hours a week to help out plus studying, and his best friend had gone to Canada.
>
> Phil had always worked hard in his studies to try to be the best he could be, and his parents said they had never put pressure on him to study because he put so much on himself!
>
> Phil always enjoyed sport, and while working and studying, the easiest physical activity to do was to go to the gym. As the stress had built up, Phil went more often. He liked how his body was responding to the gym, and he started eating less fat and carbohydrates in his diet, and more protein to assist. He lost weight and the more he lost the more control he felt in his life.
>
> Initially his mood was good, but in recent months he had felt down. He also felt anxious about his mother and his grades. His strategies of eating less and exercising more seemed to help him cope, but now he felt trapped by them.
>
> Phil's parents were increasingly worried about him and insisted he go to a doctor for a check-up. Phil was reluctant but agreed in the end to keep his mother happy.

With eating disorders, a thorough medical assessment (including blood tests) is needed to assess nutritional status and vital signs such as blood pressure. When there are concerns about physical safety, a hospital admission may be required to stabilize the person medically and reverse the effects of starvation.

A psychological and psychiatric assessment will also be needed. The man's history in childhood and school, family and partner relationships and work history will be talked about, along with any history of trauma. Treatment will involve:

- A team approach, with doctors and therapists. Note that trusting relationships are vital.
- Education about eating disorders.
- Self-help programs if the issues are mild.
- Ongoing medical checks as well as psychological and/or psychiatric treatment.
- Talking therapies such as family therapy (for children and young people), interpersonal therapy and cognitive behaviour therapy.
- Work on self-confidence and social skills, such as assertiveness.
- Teaching coping skills (e.g. problem-solving), and emotion regulation. Dialectical behaviour therapy may be helpful (see page 183).
- Addressing body image issues and dissatisfaction.
- Treatment of related anxiety, depression, personality or substance-related issues (see chapters 3, 4 and 5).
- Possibly medication.
- Hospital programs if the issues are more severe.
- Outpatient treatment programs at specialized centres.
- Support for family and carers.

Phil saw the doctor and over a few appointments gained some trust in him. All of his vital signs and blood tests were normal, and the doctor suggested that he come back and see him to keep an eye on his weight and wellbeing. Phil reluctantly agreed.

The doctor was also adamant that Phil see a nutritionist and a therapist, both of whom specialized in helping individuals with

*eating-related issues. Phil skipped the first appointment, but
when the therapist called, he felt guilty and went to the next one.*

*Over time Phil engaged in therapy and came to understand
that all of the stress and the expectations he had of himself
had contributed to the issues he was having with eating and
over-exercising. The therapist guided him through cognitive
behaviour therapy specifically for eating disorders and also
addressed body image issues of concern. It would be quite a long
road back to health, but Phil made steady progress over time.*

If you are a family member, friend or carer, and are worried a
male you know may have an eating disorder, aim to help him feel
safe in talking about the issues. Be supportive and if they don't
wish to talk with you, help them to find someone they can talk to.
Learn as much as you can about eating disorders beforehand and
choose a private place to approach them. Be kind and empathetic
and discuss your concerns.

As mentioned earlier, eating disorders can result in severe
illness or death. Here are some tips from Mental Health First Aid
Australia about when to seek emergency assistance (see also the
Resources section at the end of the book).

WHEN TO SEEK EMERGENCY ASSISTANCE FOR A MALE WITH AN EATING DISORDER

- If they have injured themselves or become suicidal.
- Their weight is too low (a Body Mass Index (BMI) less than 16).
- You note they are confused or disoriented.
- There are fainting spells, or they are feeling very cold or weak.

- There are painful muscle spasms or an irregular heartbeat.
- They are experiencing trouble breathing or having chest pain.

BODY DYSMORPHIA

Men with body dysmorphia worry a great deal about how they look. They may become preoccupied with one or more features of their body that are either not present or only slightly present. This leads to frequently checking their appearance and seeking reassurance.

Men with body dysmorphia may focus on their hair (baldness), skin, muscle size and tone, and genitalia (penis size). They may groom excessively, try to hide the perceived problem, pick at their skin or have cosmetic treatments, including surgery, when they are not needed.

There can be significant issues with self-worth, body image and shame associated with this disorder. Thinking and behaviours are often obsessional, and anxiety and depression, or suicidal thinking, can result. You can see how images of the 'ideal male' in the media may contribute to the development of this disorder.

We know that more males are suffering from body dysmorphia and, in particular, a type called 'muscle dysmorphia' (you may see it referred to as 'bigorexia'). This can lead to excessive exercise, anxiety if unable to work out, compulsive comparing to other men, mood swings, or using harmful diets or drugs (steroids, peptides). A range of treatments are available, including:

- education about the issues
- support groups

- talking therapies such as cognitive behaviour therapy
- skills to manage anxiety and depression
- learning various coping skills
- improving self-belief and self-confidence
- medication, if needed.

Check out the following tips for managing body dysmorphia for those with the disorder, and for family or carers (see also Resources section at the end of the book).

TIPS FOR MANAGING BODY DYSMORPHIA
- Drop comparisons with other people.
- Look after your body and focus on eating and exercise for health and wellbeing.
- Focus on the parts of yourself you do like.
- Don't try to be someone else or exercise your way to look like someone else.
- Remember photos on social media or in magazines are manipulated and photoshopped; the person often does not actually look like that.
- There is much more to you than the way you look. You have many strengths and resources.[4]

For family and carers:
- Recognize this is a disorder and avoid judgement and blame.
- Provide emotional support and encourage the man to seek help.
- Avoid blaming yourself or taking things personally.
- Don't support the false beliefs by reassuring the person over and over again, don't participate in

checking behaviours or assist the person to find unnecessary solutions to their concern (e.g. finding out details of surgery).

- Be encouraging and help the man not avoid activities.
- Look after yourself too and seek support if needed.
- If you are concerned about depression or suicide, assist the person to seek help immediately.

PSYCHOSIS

The term 'psychosis' refers to losing contact with reality. There are many causes of psychosis, but the main ones are schizophrenia and drug-induced psychosis. Schizophrenia has a usual onset in the early twenties, affects 1 per cent of men, and is mostly a long-term issue. There can be high levels of depression and loss of social functioning with schizophrenia; however, it is treatable and many people lead fulfilling lives. Drug-induced psychosis is due to recreational drugs (hallucinogens, amphetamines, stimulants) and mostly stops when the drugs are gone. The main symptoms of psychosis are:

- Changes in emotion and motivation (depression, anxiety, irritability, suspiciousness, blunted emotion, reduced motivation.
- Changes in thinking and perception, including reduced concentration, interrupted trains of thought, a sense of alteration of self or others, fixed ideas that are unusual (e.g. people conspiring against you), or hallucinations (often auditory, that is, hearing things that are not real, or visual, that is, seeing things that are not present).
- Changes to behaviour, such as sleep disturbances, social isolation or agitation.

The treatment of psychosis involves:

- Early intervention and taking a whole person approach.
- Having a thorough treatment plan worked out collaboratively with your doctor.
- Education about the condition and potential causes and treatments.
- Support.
- Improving lifestyle, including diet, exercise, sleep and activity levels.
- Managing stress.
- Talking therapies such as counselling and cognitive behaviour therapy.
- Working with loss and grief and sense of self-worth/ identity.
- Working closely with families.
- Group programs (e.g. focusing on managing hallucinations, mood issues and life skills).
- Social skills training.
- Fostering involvement in the community (e.g. gym programs, group programs).
- Assistance with housing, finances.
- Treatment of associated issues, such as depression or substance use (see chapters 4 and 5).
- Monitoring physical health and wellbeing.
- Maintaining hope and focusing on recovery.
- Having a relapse prevention plan (see page 130).
- Suicide prevention via appropriate treatment and support.
- Medication (antipsychotics, mood stabilizers).
- Support for families or carers.

TIP: Early treatment in psychosis is vital and improves later outcomes. Seek help early from your doctor or a mental health team.

It is known that men experiencing psychotic symptoms may not reach out for help. The symptoms can trigger shame or fear. If you are a friend, colleague or family member concerned that the man is experiencing psychosis, then be empathetic and speak to them privately about their experiences.

It is important not to be confrontational and to communicate in an uncomplicated and clear way. Focus on listening and do not think that you have to talk the man out of particular ideas. And if he does not want to talk, then do not force the issue, but let him know that you are there if he wants to talk in the future. It is also useful to let him know that there is professional help available.

There is greater risk of self-harm and suicide when psychosis is present, so refer to Chapter 10 about how to respond. The disturbances to perception (hallucinations) in particular can trigger aggression at times and, if this is present, it is important to stay calm, speak quietly, and not restrict the person's movement. Never put yourself at risk and seek help if need be (a mental health team or emergency services).

At times the person with psychosis (or another impairing mental health condition) will be compulsorily detained (or sectioned) at a hospital for assessment and treatment. This occurs when that person needs immediate treatment, which cannot be provided adequately in other settings, and they are at risk to themselves or another person. Detention occurs when the person does not agree to be voluntarily admitted, usually related to a lack of insight due to illness. Two professionals must assess the person as needing to be kept in hospital for a period of time. The aim is to ensure the person is safe and receives the treatment they need (see also the Resources section at the end of the book).

DEMENTIA

Dementia is a term for a group of disorders affecting the brain. It describes a collection of symptoms for which the cause can vary greatly. Most men with dementia are older, but it can occur in younger men from their forties. Dementia is a common cause of hospital admissions and death in older men throughout the world. About 50 million people worldwide have dementia.

KEY POINT

Dementia mainly affects older people, but it is not a normal part of ageing.

The most common types of dementia are Alzheimer's disease, vascular dementia (due to problems with blood flow in the brain), Lewy body disease (loss of nerve cells in the brain due to abnormal protein deposits called 'Lewy bodies'), frontotemporal dementia (referring to particular parts of the brain that deteriorate), and alcohol-related dementia.

The early signs of dementia are memory loss (progressive or frequent), confusion, personality change, apathy and withdrawing socially, and loss of ability to perform everyday tasks (see Resources section at the end of the book).

It is important to have a careful assessment by your doctor or a geriatrician, as some medical conditions can mimic dementia (e.g. depression, low thyroid, some vitamin deficiencies, over-medication, brain tumours). The treatment of dementia includes:

- education about dementia and its treatment
- support groups
- counselling for the man and their family
- working through loss and grief
- stimulating cognition (memory, attention) and activity
- practical guidance about planning ahead about money and powers of attorney
- assistance with advance care directives (related to wishes in relation to future health care and end of life), which need to be put in place in case legal capacity is lost
- strategies for reducing stress and anxiety (e.g. relaxation tools, responding calmly and providing reassurance)
- improving lifestyle (e.g. healthy diet, healthy weight, quitting smoking, reducing caffeine, regular exercise)
- looking after physical health by seeing a doctor regularly and managing conditions, like diabetes and hearing loss
- drug treatments
- treating related symptoms (e.g. depression, sleeplessness, agitation)
- support for family or carers (online forums, seeing a doctor or counsellor, phone support, support groups) or respite.

WHAT WE HAVE LOOKED AT SO FAR!

A common thread is the importance of a thorough and early assessment when faced with a mental health disorder. It is important to ensure the issue is identified and appropriate treatment can be undertaken. With all of the issues, understanding the disorder(s) and possible treatments, and having a thorough treatment plan are vital.

There are excellent sources of information available for the man affected, and for his family or carers, specifically good online resources, books, community groups and services.

Maintaining hope and focusing on recovery are vital, and there are many practical tools which can assist. We encourage you to seek out more information from the resources at the end of the book or seek support from your doctor and local services.

10.

PREVENTING SUICIDE AND DEALING WITH NON-SUICIDAL SELF-HARM

What lies behind us and what lies before us are tiny matters compared to what lies within us.

Ralph Waldo Emerson

Too many men are suffering in silence and dying from suicide. Every year a significant number of suicide deaths occur worldwide with over 3000 each year in Australia, 47,000 in the USA and 6000 in the United Kingdom. Many of these deaths relate to men.[1]

This chapter focuses on the prevention of suicidal behaviours and non-suicidal self-harm (behaviours deliberately hurting the body, such as cutting). It is written both for the man who may be experiencing distress, or for someone who is trying to assist him. It offers information and some tools to assist, but these do not replace emergency support or professional assistance. So, if you are struggling, don't wait! Please seek help straight away.

At the centre of all crises is suffering. Suicidal thoughts and behaviours may be motivated by the desire to escape or relieve distressing feelings or situations, or to communicate feelings or change how other people are responding.[2]

Having suicidal thoughts or behaviours, or non-suicidal self-harm, is invariably very stressful and distressing, but please know that there is always hope and whatever the situation is, it *can* improve. You have many strengths and resources within yourself to draw on and help is available. Here is Roger's story:

> Roger is a 50-year-old bookkeeper who has had a bout of severe depression. He has had depression in the past as well. Life has been challenging recently with work and marital problems.
>
> Roger's father lives overseas and his mother died a few years ago. He lost a younger brother in a tragic accident, which he witnessed as a child. The depression has been 'paralyzing' and Roger has been struggling with suicidal thoughts.

SUICIDE PREVENTION

There are many programs aimed at preventing suicide. There are those at a society level that work to reduce the stigma around suicide, to prevent trauma and to improve access to healthcare and media reporting guidelines. There are tailored programs for high-risk groups in the community, such as veterans, refugees or the bereaved, and there are programs offering treatment and support for individuals, to ensure their safety and provide psychological assistance to address any underlying or current issues.

In this chapter, we are going to look at a few suicide prevention strategies, namely:

- Mental health first aid (just like a physical injury, a mental health crisis, such as suicidal thinking, requires first aid).

- Having access to information.
- Reaching out for help.

And we will finish with help for the family.

Mental health first aid

Excellent mental health first aid training and resources are now available. These help you offer assistance to a man who is experiencing suicidal thoughts, before they are able to access professional help.

Based on the work of Mental Health First Aid Australia, if you are concerned that someone is suicidal, watch for these signals or signs:

- Threats of suicide, searching for ways to kill themselves (e.g. online searches, looking for weapons), talking about death or suicide, expressing hopelessness, anger, revenge seeking, and acting recklessly.
- Saying they are trapped or there is 'no way out', or that there is no reason for living or no sense of purpose in life.
- Increasing alcohol or drug use, withdrawal from family or friends, signs of anxiety or depression, inability to sleep, dramatic changes in mood (including a sudden improvement in mood or calmness).

And, if you think someone is suicidal:

- Tell them you are worried, and that you care.
- Express empathy for them and what they are going through.

- Talk in a matter-of-fact way — there is no need to skirt around things.
- Ask directly whether they are suicidal (e.g. 'Are you having thoughts of suicide? Are you thinking about killing yourself?').
- Let them know suicidal thoughts are common and can be associated with treatable mental health issues.
- Tell them they need to get help and offer to assist with this.
- Get them to ring a crisis service or assist with this.[3]

If you think the person might be at the point of ending their life, indicated by them saying they have decided how or when to kill themselves, that they have access to the means to take their life, or that they are more at risk due to past behaviours or substance use, *do not* leave them alone and call the emergency services.

KEY POINT

To help a person who you think is suicidal, tell them you are worried and that you care, ask them if they are suicidal, do not leave them alone, and assist them to get help (emergency services).

Having access to information

Having information is very important, as it debunks some myths about suicide and empowers you. So, let's have a look at some information related to suicide prevention:

- Overall, between 1 to 2 per cent of deaths are by suicide and men account for 70 per cent of suicides.[4]

- The greatest risk of suicide is in the mid-forties and over 80 years of age.
- Indigenous people and individuals identifying as gay, trans-sexual or with another gender or sexual identity are at a higher risk.

Rates of suicide are higher in men than women. This may be explained by men's reluctance to acknowledge problems or seek help. It is also suggested that, although men and women experience depression in a similar way, they have different ways of expressing their distress. Men are more likely to be overwhelmed after a longer period of suffering and release the emotion in the form of anger and violence, often directed at themselves. This is in contrast to women, who are more prepared to release emotions early by crying and seeking help.

There are many risk factors for suicidal behaviours, including:

- A previous suicide attempt.
- Mental health issues, especially depression, bipolar disorder, schizophrenia and substance-related issues.
- A recent discharge from a psychiatric hospital.
- Physical illness, especially if terminal, painful or debilitating.
- A family history of suicide or substance-related or mental health issues.
- A history of bullying, trauma or abuse.
- Being socially isolated.
- A tendency to be impulsive.
- Recent exposure to suicide of someone else.
- Loss and grief.
- Family problems.

- Unemployment or any changes to employment and not being able to provide for the family (and feeling like a 'failure').
- Rejection by a significant person.
- Relationship breakdown and divorce.
- Poverty.
- A sense of hopelessness, particularly from social issues or depression.[5,6]

Mental health stigma in the community and lack of adequate health services also contribute. Men in certain occupations are more at risk, such as military members and farmers. It is also suggested that modern media (films, social media) may influence rates of suicide, but also some media may assist help-seeking.

Reaching out for help

When an individual man is having suicidal thoughts or there have been suicidal behaviours, it is important to seek help. Depending on the issues, help may be sought from emergency services, crisis or mental health services or a doctor or therapist. The most important thing is that whomever is struggling is helped to feel safe and has the opportunity to talk.

KEY POINT

Suicidal thoughts or behaviours are often very distressing (they can be frightening and associated with a sense of shame), so there will be relief at being able to talk about what is happening.

Doctors and mental health professionals will:

- Assess the degree of risk with the aim of differentiating those who face low risk versus those who face high risk and who may attempt suicide.
- Manage any risk so that help can be provided to stave off suicide attempts.
- Take into account risk factors and protective factors (such as family support).
- Check out thoughts about suicide and how long these have been present (e.g. any threats, plans or preparations, recent or past suicidal behaviours).
- Investigate any mental health issues, level of functioning day to day, any substance use, social supports or other resources.

They will ask questions like:

- Do you ever feel like giving up?
- How does the future seem to you?
- Does your life ever seem so bad that you wish to die?
- How severe are the thoughts? How frequent?
- Have you made any plans?
- How close have you come to doing something?
- What stops you doing something?[7]

In general, increases in frequency, intensity and duration of suicidal behaviour are an indicator of how severe the issue is. There is great concern when the man is saying that they have no reason to live, are a burden to others, or are in unbearable pain. A change in behaviours, such as more risk-taking behaviours, substance use, withdrawing from people and activities, sorting out personal affairs or giving away possessions can also indicate increasing risk.

The level of care that is needed will be considered. You may be able to manage yourself with some phone support, or care may be provided by family and a local doctor. As risk increases more support is needed from mental health services, a therapist or psychiatrist. Sometimes an immediate referral to a hospital for further assessment, and possibly admission to ensure safety, may be needed.

A safety plan may be helpful for individuals. This involves writing a plan when feeling calm and writing about warning signs of a crisis, creating a safe place, people who can be contacted as well as professional help. The Australian organization Beyond Blue has developed 'Beyond Now', a suicide safety planning app for smartphones that provides a helpful way for people to develop a personalized safety plan. Information can be found at www.beyondblue.org.au/get-support/beyondnow-suicide-safety-planning.

When individual treatment is needed, it will focus on:

- Support and listening.
- Problem-solving any worrying issues and learning new problem-solving skills (see Chapter 2).
- Developing self-awareness of thoughts, feelings and strengths.
- Dealing with unhelpful thoughts or underlying beliefs through cognitive behaviour therapy (see Chapter 4). See the exercise 'Dealing with suicidal thoughts' on the next page, as this involves working with thoughts.
- Dealing with uncomfortable emotions (e.g. guilt or shame). Learning to tolerate distress and regulate emotions (see Chapter 6).
- Using a principle from dialectical behaviour therapy that we can have opposing thoughts and motivations

(e.g. a desire to end life but to also seek help and live). The therapy builds on the desire to live and the reasons for this.

- Assistance with any interpersonal issues (e.g. conflict, relationship breakdown, bullying).
- Loss and grief counselling.
- Narrative therapy and identifying the person's resources and strengths (see Chapter 4).
- Dealing with substance-related issues, including motivational therapy (refer to Chapter 5).

Learning how to deal with painful feelings and thoughts is vital. Suicidal thinking or behaviours may be attempts to solve problems that seem intolerable or to escape painful feelings. Therapy needs to address problem-solving and how to tolerate the feelings.

DEALING WITH SUICIDAL THOUGHTS

We actually have 'suicidal thoughts' rather than 'feeling suicidal' (the feeling may be depression, anger or despair). Often these thoughts are really distressing and overwhelming, but it is important to recognize that they are thoughts only and may not be based on truth.

It is important to be aware of the thoughts and to understand that they may be driven by depressed mood or recent events, and to know that you can deal with the thoughts in different ways. You can challenge them, 'Am I catastrophizing the situation, or seeing it more bleakly than it is?', 'Is there another way to think about things?', or you can observe them and let them pass. (See chapters 2 and 4 for more information on these approaches to thoughts, and work with your doctor or therapist).

Help for the family or significant others

Family members affected by a person's suicidal thinking or behaviours also need support and assistance. Seeking out help from your doctor is a good place to start. They can talk to you and provide support and assistance, as well as organize a referral for specialist assistance if needed.

If the person has been harmed or has died, there will be significant trauma and many distressing emotions. Assistance will most likely be needed, so please seek some support and help, maybe starting with your doctor (see also the Resources section at the end of the book).

NON-SUICIDAL SELF-HARM

This section covers non-suicidal self-harm, which means inflicting damage to one's own body without the intention of suicide (and not consistent with cultural norms).[8] We will look at some facts about these behaviours, mental health first aid, and strategies which can help (see also the Resources section at the end of the book).

The most common methods of non-suicidal self-harm are cutting (70 per cent) or scratching, deliberately hitting the body on a hard surface, punching, hitting or slapping one's self, and biting or burning. Burning or self-battery are more common in males.

Non-suicidal self-harm is common in adolescents and young adults. The lifetime rates in these groups are 15 to 20 per cent, with the onset typically at 13 to 14 years of age. Occurrence is highest in individuals with mental health issues, such as depression and anxiety, or those who struggle to regulate their emotions or those who are highly self-critical. About 6 per cent of adults report non-suicidal self-harm.[9] The reasons for these behaviours are reported to be to:

- manage painful or overwhelming feelings
- punish oneself
- communicate with others, or
- for other reasons (e.g. feeling emotionally numb).

Remember that most men feel ashamed of the behaviours and are not seeking attention. They are at a higher risk of suicide. In fact, it has been found that 10 per cent of people who had injured themselves in the past four weeks had made a suicide attempt in the last year, and 60 per cent had thoughts of suicide.[10]

Mental health first aid

Don't assume that those who self-harm are suicidal, and don't presume they are not. The only way to know is to ask them (see the previous section on suicide prevention).

If you suspect someone is self-harming, then discuss it with them if you feel able to, in a private place. You might say something like, 'Sometimes when people are in a lot of emotional pain, they injure themselves on purpose. Is that how your injury happened?'

Reaching out for help

If you interrupt someone who is injuring themselves, be calm and intervene in a supportive and non-judgemental way. Tell them you are concerned and ask if you can provide support. Organize medical help if needed. When talking with them express empathy, listen to them, validate their feelings or concerns, give support and reassurance that there is help available, don't promise to keep the behaviour a secret, and encourage them to seek professional help (from a doctor or mental health professional), and assist them to do so if they ask you.

> ## KEY POINT
>
> If the self-harm is severe, interfering with functioning, or if the person has injured their eyes or genitals, or expressed a desire to die, contact the emergency services immediately.

When an individual who has been self-harming seeks help from a therapist, they will focus on increasing healthy coping skills rather than removing unhealthy ones. This will involve learning self-soothing and emotion regulation skills as outlined in Chapter 6, as well as strategies to effectively communicate their needs (see Chapter 4).

ALTERNATIVES TO SELF-HARM
- Talk to someone (e.g. family, friend, helpline).
- Delay (the urge to self-harm will pass).
- Wait 5 minutes, then wait another 5 minutes more.
- Count from 1 to 100 or do some breathing exercises (see Chapter 3).
- Make the environment safe (e.g. make sure sharp objects are removed).
- Go to a different spot in the house or change your environment (e.g. go for a walk).
- Use a distraction (e.g. watch a film, play video games, do some exercise, or make a self-harm distraction box with things to concentrate on).

- Do something like holding a piece of ice or touch different textures around you.
- Have a cry.
- Write in a journal.
- If you need to see blood, then draw on the skin with a red pen.
- If you feel the need to punish yourself, then instead look for a way to forgive or be kind to yourself.
- If you feel overwhelmed and need to express anger, then punch a pillow or a punching bag.
- Avoid any activities that harm you or cause pain. In this way the brain will stop associating physical pain with relief or feeling good.[11, 12]

WHAT WE HAVE LOOKED AT SO FAR!

Suicide and non-suicidal self-harm are far too common. Those who are struggling with mental health issues or are feeling overwhelmed by their emotions are more at risk. Let's hear more about Roger:

Roger shared his worrying thoughts with his wife and she organized an appointment for him to see his doctor urgently. His thoughts were very distressing and it was good to talk about them to the doctor.

The doctor spent time with Roger and they came to the decision that although Roger had many thoughts, he was low risk at that time because there were a number of protective factors, such as family. Despite the marital issues, Roger's wife had continued being very supportive and she was with Roger most of the time.

The doctor and Roger reviewed his treatment plan and modified the medication being taken. He also contacted Roger's therapist and organized an urgent review, plus a referral was made to a psychiatrist.

An appointment was made two days later with the doctor again to monitor Roger's mood and suicidal risk. Roger and his wife were given phone numbers to contact at any time for assistance.

We have seen in this chapter that the mental health first aid guidelines offer excellent ideas on how to assist a man who is at risk of suicide. The key is to be empathic and listen, and to speak matter-of-factly. You don't need to walk on eggshells around someone who is struggling.

If you ask clear questions, then you are likely to get clear answers. It is better to be wrong and someone say, 'No, I'm not suicidal (or) harming myself,' than to be silent. And if you think someone is suicidal or is self-harming themselves severely, contact the emergency services. Doctors and mental health professionals can assess someone who is having suicidal thoughts or injuring themselves and provide the tools for coping with these thoughts or behaviours. They can also assist with any related issues, such as trauma or depression. Help is available, so please reach out, if need be.

11.

PREVENTING MENTAL HEALTH ISSUES AND FOSTERING SELF-BELIEF

The purpose of life is a life of purpose.
Robert Byrne

Prevention is about stopping something from happening and, in terms of mental health, it is about preventing the occurrence of an issue in the first place or preventing it from worsening or recurring. And if it is a long-lasting issue, then learning to manage it, and having the best quality of life possible.

Many of the tools and exercises in this book aim to help you build coping skills (mindfulness), improve the current circumstances in your life (doing regular exercise, reassessing your lifestyle), and prevent issues from occurring in the first place or relapsing (seeing a doctor or therapist). All of these tools are ultimately related to prevention.

A number of key tools to improve mental health and wellbeing were provided in Chapter 2, one of which was related directly to prevention. You might like to go back and read the section on prevention in Chapter 2, as well as the section on improving your lifestyle and reducing stress in Chapter 3, as these are other important prevention tools too.

Many of the tools discussed in this book have the bonus of building your sense of self-belief and resilience. We will look at self-belief a little later in the chapter but, in relation to resilience, we often hear that it refers to the ability 'to bounce back'. In other words, it is about adapting to stress and change in life.

To further understand resilience, the metaphor of a bridge is helpful, in which stressors create a load on the bridge and the pillars of the bridge (your personal resources) give it strength. When faced with demands in life, individuals who are more resilient will worry less and keep functioning even when life is stressful and tough.

KEY POINT

Resilience is about adapting to the demands and challenges in life. Greater resilience leads to less worry and better functioning when life is stressful.

Another important concept in relation to prevention is learning to relate to emotions differently and regulate them. We addressed these ideas in Chapter 6 when talking about working with uncomfortable feelings, such as anger and grief. Many of the tools highlighted in chapters 3 and 4 can also help manage emotions and build emotional intelligence. We will explore this form of intelligence more in this chapter. In addition, Chapter 5 on substance-related issues, and Chapter 10 on suicide and self-harm, had prevention as a focus.

So, make prevention a priority in your life. You already have knowledge of prevention and, with the tools already in your toolkit, you have many ways to protect your mental health and reduce the risk of mental health issues occurring or worsening. To assist you, in this chapter we will look at some other important aspects of prevention and building resilience (see also the Resources section at the end of the book).

PREVENTION

As a society, we need to focus on preventing mental health issues occurring in the first place. There are many aspects to this, including reducing the stigma around mental health issues, preventing trauma and improving access to health care.

At the centre of this for men is tackling some of society's ideas and stereotypes about what it is to be a man. Connor Beaton did an excellent TEDx Talk on 'The Mask of Masculinity'. He said that society needs to overcome the negative stereotypes surrounding masculinity, particularly one that says men have to be macho, as this promotes the idea that the highest value of men is to dominate, control and succeed at all costs. Beaton speaks of men wearing 'the mask of masculinity', which means that 'real men' don't cry or express emotions (unless it is anger), they don't show empathy, they show their strength with retaliation, and they are tough. He says that the consequences of this mask are the increasing rates of suicide in men. He also speaks of the isolation of men, that 50 per cent of men cannot identify a close friend to turn to when times are tough.

Another stereotype that we need to work on is that it is 'weak' to seek help. We need to overcome the barriers to getting some help and part of this is understanding shame and learning that it is okay to be vulnerable.

Policy makers and individual health practices need to recognize that there is not one type of masculinity, and that we need different ways of engaging men and meeting their needs. Education is also needed across the community about men's mental health and wellbeing.

We also need to challenge the idea that men are not interested in their health and wellbeing and address men's issues related to lifestyle, stress, relationships and work, and possibly work on managing anger or risk-taking (e.g. substance use). Most of these topics have been addressed in this book.

TIP: When you are going to ask for some help, it can be useful to write down your concerns. Make a list or make some notes to assist you in explaining the issues. You might give it to a doctor or mental health professional to read.

There is an interesting paradox in our society. We know that average incomes have increased substantially in the western world over the past 50 years but increases in material wealth have not increased our happiness at all! Rates of depression are higher than ever. Part of this is thought to be related to the human tendency to compare ourselves to others and, in the western world, we are caught on a treadmill of comparisons about what others look like, what they do and what they own.[1]

So how do we get off the treadmill, feel better about ourselves and prevent mental health problems from arising? One way is to keep building our emotional intelligence, or our ability to recognize and manage our emotions. We looked at ways of managing emotions such as shame and anger in Chapter 6, and here are some general tips for developing your emotional intelligence.

HOW TO DEVELOP GREATER EMOTIONAL INTELLIGENCE

- Be aware of the sensations in your body related to the emotion (e.g. anger might trigger muscle tension, or sadness might be felt in the chest).
- Name the feelings or put words to them.
- Know that expressing feelings is a learnt behaviour, so practice is needed to get good at expressing feelings.
- Give yourself permission to show some vulnerability.
- Learn to manage your emotions, in particular to soothe distressing emotions.
- Ask for help when you need it.[2]

Another means of preventing mental health issues is to adopt the positive psychology approach, which focuses on human strengths and wellbeing and aims to help people achieve their optimal health and wellbeing. Positive psychology achieves this by focusing on PERMA:

Positive emotions (such as joy or love)

Engagement in life and activities

Relationships

Meaning in life, and

Accomplishment.

We mentioned in Chapter 2 that PERMA involves a whole lot of factors. We have already looked at a number of them in previous chapters, but let's look at a few key ones here.

Connection

There is a lot of evidence that connection with others is important to mental health and wellbeing. A Harvard study has shown that people who are more socially connected to family, friends and the community live happier, healthier and longer lives than those who are less connected.[3] Danish and Australian researchers also found that in older people, increasing engagement with social or leisure activities reduced the chance of depression, as well as anxiety and dementia. Equally, being involved in social networks was helpful.[4] Following this study, the research team came up with a model called Act–Belong–Commit (ABC):

ACT = actively engage in social and recreational activities.

BELONG = keep up friendships, be involved with others in groups/activities.

COMMIT = do things that provide meaning and purpose.

This model can provide a prevention framework. Think about where some current challenges are for you in following this model. For example, men tend to let go of friendships as they settle with a partner and focus on family responsibilities, and social isolation can be a significant issue for men in their middle years after divorce, or for older men post-retirement. Try the following exercise.

ACT–BELONG–COMMIT
Can you identify any challenges to putting ABC into action? How can you overcome these challenges? (Using the problem-solving exercise on pages 70–71 might help with this). Consider setting some goals around ABC (see page 25).

Author Steve Biddulph reminds men to develop their communication skills to help build friendships. He talks about different levels of communication, from sharing facts about the world and yourself, to past feelings and current feelings. A strong friendship means that you can share more of these levels with them.[5]

Remember, too, that men need the support of other men when there are mental health issues pushing them around. So, consider whether you can develop more friendships or become involved in community-based men's groups or treatment groups.

Values

The concept of values has come up a number of times in the book. This is because it is an important one — when we live a life that fits with our values, we feel happier and have a more fulfilling life. Revisit the section on values in Chapter 2, or you might like to explore values in a different way here.

Consider your key life areas and rate each one out of 10 (with 1 being 'very poorly' to 10 being 'as well as it could'). Then think of three ways you could improve your score over the next month and write them down. Don't forget to break these down into small steps to act on over the month, then score the areas again at the end of the month. Remember that any improvement in score is good, even one point!

ANOTHER VALUES EXERCISE

Life area	Rate what you think about the area now (1 to 10)	List three ways you can improve your score over the next month (remember to take small steps)	Rate what you think about the area in a month (1 to 10)
Health and wellbeing			
Family and friends			
Partner relationships			
Work/finances			
Education/self-development			

Life area	Rate what you think about the area now (1 to 10)	List three ways you can improve your score over the next month (remember to take small steps)	Rate what you think about the area in a month (1 to 10)
Leisure			
Community			
Environment			
Spirituality			

Purpose

Purpose refers to the reason why we do things or why they exist. The Japanese refer to it as *ikigai* or 'a reason for being'. So why is purpose so important? 'Blue zones' refer to areas in the world where people live the longest. The characteristics of these areas have been studied and, apart from healthy lifestyles, the importance of social connection and a sense of life purpose are recognized.[6] Also, those who identify a source of purpose and meaning in their lives report greater happiness and life satisfaction, greater health, more resilience, and a greater sense of control.

Humans thrive on a sense of purpose as it gives them meaning in life. Jewish psychiatrist Viktor Frankl, who was sent to a concentration camp in Europe during World War II, has suggested that to understand our meaning and purpose, we must know ourselves and focus on something bigger than ourselves (e.g. service to others or the environment). This is why identifying what you believe in is important (values, beliefs), so that you can understand your life purpose. Here are some tips to help you find your sense of purpose.

TEN TIPS TO HELP YOU FIND A GREATER SENSE OF PURPOSE

1. Give yourself permission to explore your purpose and reflect on this.
2. Go back to your values as these can guide your purpose (see Chapter 2).
3. Be aware of thoughts which block your sense of purpose (e.g. 'I couldn't do that', see Chapter 4).
4. Be less self-critical (see Chapter 4).
5. Utilize any passions you have (e.g. music, helping others, gardening), as purpose is about doing what we love and were meant to do.
6. We all have strengths and gifts, so we can get closer to our purpose when we use them (see Chapter 2).

7. Build your self-belief.
8. Grow relationships and connections.
9. Consider further training or mentoring and apply effort.
10. Trust in your abilities and your intuition about your purpose.

Kindness

Kindness can assist others and lift your own spirits. Not only does it feel good, but there is also growing evidence that being kind can help your mental and physical wellbeing. We know that being kind results in the production of the hormone oxytocin, which helps us feel relaxed and happy. Oxytocin is good for our physical health too, as it lowers blood pressure.

Engaging in random acts of kindness can often lead you to feeling more connected with others and more empathic. As social creatures, this is important. Kindness is associated with feeling more positive too.

Researcher Barbara Frederickson has done a lot of work in the area of positivity. She describes how a 'loving-kindness meditation', based on ancient Buddhist practices, fosters positive emotions.

LOVING-KINDNESS MEDITATION
Meditate on this ancient Tibetan Buddhist poem on
loving-kindness:

May I be filled with loving-kindness
May I be well
May I be peaceful and at ease
May I be happy.

Focus on warm and compassionate feelings in your heart area.
You can direct these feelings to yourself in your meditation, and
then to an ever-widening circle of others!

Kindness is closely related to compassion, which is about empathy for the suffering of others. It means that you offer understanding and kindness to others when they make mistakes or fail, rather than judging them harshly. Acceptance and being non-judgemental are important aspects of compassion.

Self-compassion is a form of kindness. It means you are able to be kind and understanding towards yourself, instead of criticizing and judging yourself harshly. One of the traps in life is comparing yourself with others, as we are hardwired to do this as part of our tools for survival. If we come across an individual who looks threatening, then comparison is important. However, much of the time we have no need to compare, and frequent comparison leads to suffering.

Alex recognizes the importance of kindness to others and, like most young men, is working on being more compassionate to himself. Here are some tips from him for practising more kindness in life.

TEN TIPS FOR BRINGING MORE KINDNESS INTO YOUR EVERYDAY LIFE

1. Say thank you often.
2. Give compliments regularly.
3. Donate some time or money to a good cause.
4. Help out a friend or family member (you can do even do this secretly!).
5. Donate blood if you can.
6. Lend a hand to someone in need (e.g. volunteer work).
7. Give someone a small gift.
8. Help someone out at work.
9. Drop comparisons to others (it may help to spend more time off social media).
10. Be more compassionate to yourself in your self-talk.

SELF-BELIEF

Many men struggle with a sense of self-worth. You may have said in your life, 'I have low self-esteem,' or you might be highly self-critical (e.g. your self-talk might include negative statements like 'I'm stupid!'). You are not born with high or low self-esteem. This actually relates to your underlying thoughts and beliefs about yourself, which develop over time. When these are more positive and helpful, they are referred to as self-belief. They drive your perception of yourself and your feeling of self-confidence, and build resilience.

Low self-belief can contribute to stress, anxiety and low mood. In turn, these can affect sleep and eating habits, or the ability to exercise. Low self-belief can affect your self-confidence and may prevent you from socializing or going to work functions. It may affect your assertiveness with others or cause you to avoid putting yourself forward for tasks at work through fear of failing. Having a strong sense of self-belief enables you to be more resilient. There are a number of influences on self-belief:

- Early life experiences: A child who experiences a lot of criticism growing up, for example, will struggle to develop a strong sense of self-belief. The child might take on the belief that he is not good enough or doesn't achieve what is expected. Experiences such as prolonged separation from parents, neglect, or emotional, physical, or sexual abuse can greatly affect a person's self-belief.

- Ongoing life experiences: Experiences in families, relationships or in the workplace continue to influence self-belief. The intimidating behaviours of a bully or abusive individual, for example, will impact self-belief. Compare these people to encouraging individuals who boost self-belief. Also, our health, negative life events such as losing a job, or experiencing the breakdown of a relationship can negatively affect our self-belief.

- The potentially positive or negative influences of various aspects of society will influence self-belief. Men might take on the idea that they must have certain attributes, such as being strong and successful. These views place pressure on yourself through comparison with an unrealistic ideal. Also, the modernization of technology and our increasing reliance on social media can cause distress, especially when measuring up against others or relying on self-validation through 'likes' and 'follows'.

If you think you have low self-belief, there are a number of simple steps you can take to boost your sense of self-belief and self-confidence (see also the Resources section at the end of the book):

1. Change unhelpful stories such as 'I am not good enough' to 'I am good enough' (see Chapter 4).
2. Make a list of your strengths and achievements and read this regularly (see Chapter 2). It may also help to write a list of what you are grateful for.
3. Focus on your values (also see Chapter 2).
4. Accept what is not within your control and take action that helps create a meaningful life.
5. Practise mindfulness as opposed to being caught up in thoughts or feelings, to increase self-compassion (see Chapter 3).
6. Focus on positive emotions and purpose, and celebrate your successes.
7. Enhance relationships and connect with others.
8. Accept compliments — just say thank you!
9. Eat healthily and exercise, stand tall and smile, and dress in a way that makes you feel good about yourself.
10. Do more of the things you enjoy. Spend time with people who make you feel good and avoid those who make you feel drained.

WHAT WE HAVE LOOKED AT SO FAR!

As a society we have a long way to go to assist men to remain healthy and well, or to recover from mental health issues. There are many tools to help prevent mental health issues, from improving lifestyle, to connecting more with others, learning skills in problem-solving, dealing with relationship issues, or managing thoughts and feelings.

A sense of self-belief and resilience help to prevent distress and mental health issues. Fortunately, you can develop both of these qualities and keep working on them throughout your life. A number of ways to build resilience have been highlighted in this chapter, and all involve working on self-awareness and continuing to learn as you go through life. Use the tools and exercises to develop more optimistic thinking and positive emotions (such as gratitude) to build your self-worth.

FINAL WORDS

Learn from yesterday, live for today,
hope for tomorrow.
Albert Einstein

Alex and I wrote this book because we saw a huge need for information and assistance for men in relation to mental health. We have also observed that men are changing and are actively seeking information and tools to improve their health and wellbeing. We wanted to encourage this and be a part of these changes.

Exploring men's mental health has been a huge task, and we have tried to cover as many topics as possible. The research for this book has confirmed our thinking that many men in the community are dealing with challenges in life and society, and many are dealing with mental health issues. We need to continue working on changing unhelpful ideas about masculinity, which impact negatively on men's mental health.

Along the way we have discussed how men can cope with the past and learn from their experiences by dealing with trauma, shame and grief and finding acceptance. We have looked at how men can live more healthily and foster hope for the future. As we have said, too many men are suffering, and more help is needed.

Each day it is important to keep in mind what is important to you, and to be mindful as often as you can, as well as using your strengths and fostering your sense of purpose. This helps give you meaning in life.

In relation to 'tomorrow' or the future, hope, or the sense that things will turn out okay, has a vital role in your general health. Hope is not wishful thinking, but more about focusing on optimistic thinking, identifying your goals and actively putting strategies in place to sustain the motivation to reach them. It is a state of mind and a learnt behaviour.

Since our focus has been on tools to assist your mental health and wellbeing, we have a couple of final strategies to share. You may decide to add them to your toolkit.

CREATE YOUR OWN MENTAL HEALTH CHECKLIST

Create your own mental health checklist based on some of the tips you have picked up from this book. This might look like:
- Have I eaten some healthy food today?
- Have I spent some time in nature?
- Do I need a rest (physically, mentally, socially or from work)?
- Have I connected with people I care about?
- Have I dropped comparisons and been kind in my self-talk?

Put up the list where you can see it and ask yourself these questions regularly.

Create your own wellbeing plan
Create your own wellbeing plan using the following headings:
- Move (e.g. walk each day).
- Connect (with others, with the community).
- Learn (e.g. keep reading).

- Notice (be more mindful).
- Give (to others, the environment, the community).[1]

As you now have quite a few tools to include under any of these headings, you might like to have a go at your own plan. It is a good idea to write down your plan and consult it regularly!

It is our hope that you have been provided with some ideas to challenge you in this book. We hope that you have found answers to some of your questions or concerns, and that you feel more able to express yourself and to reach out for some help if need be. Well done for working through this manual, and please be confident that you now have many more tools in your toolkit to use in dealing with mental health issues, and in life generally.

Thank you, and we wish you all the best in your life!

RESOURCES

1. ABOUT MEN'S MENTAL HEALTH

Here are a few websites with good information on men's health:

- Australia: Beacon website (beacon.anu.edu.au) is an excellent mental and physical health information portal, Head to Health (www.headtohealth.gov.au) for information and locating digital mental health resources.
- USA: National Institute of Mental Health has comprehensive information (www.nimh.nih.gov/health/topics/depression/index.shtml).
- New Zealand: Mental health information and resources (https://www.mentalhealth.org.nz/get-help/a-z).
- United Kingdom: Mental Health Foundation (www.mentalhealth.org.uk), Heads Together (www.headstogether.org.uk) brings together a team of charities working on mental health issues.

2 TWELVE KEY TOOLS TO IMPROVE YOUR MENTAL HEALTH

Work–life integration: To find out more about work–life integration read *Switch Off: How to find calm in a noisy world* by Angela Lockwood (John Wiley & Sons Australia Ltd, 2017).

Reaching out: There are many useful online resources which can give you some information about available services. And if multicultural information is needed, check out:

- Australia: Beyond Blue website (www.beyondblue.org.au/who-does-it-affect/multicultural-people).

- Canada: Multicultural Mental Health Centre (www.multiculturalmentalhealth.ca/en/consumers/getting-help/).
- United Kingdom: Mental Health Foundation (www.mentalhealth.org.uk).

Work on prevention: To find out more about positive psychology, read Martin Seligman's book *Flourish* (William Heinemann, 2012).

Kessler Psychological Distress Scale (K10): An online version of the K10 is available on the Beyond Blue website (www.beyondblue.org.au/the-facts/anxiety-and-depression-checklist-k10). You can complete it and a score will be provided. The K10 is also available in various languages at www.hcp.med.harvard.edu/ncs/k6_scales.php.

3. TACKLING STRESS AND ANXIETY

Avoidance and cognitive behaviour therapy
Books:
- Edelman, S. (2013). *Change Your Thinking: Positive and practical ways to overcome stress, negative emotions and self-defeating behaviour using CBT*, HarperCollins Publishing, Sydney.
- Kennerley, H. (2014). *Overcoming Anxiety: A self-help guide using cognitive behavioural techniques*, Little, Brown Group, London.

Websites:
- The Centre for Clinical Interventions (www.cci.health.wa.gov.au).

And you can find out more about the Yerkes-Dodson Law on YouTube (https://www.youtube.com/watch?v=8CA6Di3ixOk).

Take action — the 'struggle switch': To find out more about the 'struggle switch', go to The Struggle Switch by Dr Russ Harris on YouTube (www.youtube.com/watch?v=rCp1l16GCXI).

Utilize self-help: There are a number of resources you can access:

Books:

- Edelman, S. (2013). *Change Your Thinking: Positive and practical ways to overcome stress, negative emotions and self-defeating behaviour using CBT*, HarperCollins Publishing, Sydney.
- Harris, R. and Aisbett, B. (2013). *The Happiness Trap Pocketbook*, Exisle Publishing, Wollombi, New South Wales.
- Kennerley, H. (2014). *Overcoming Anxiety: A self-help guide using cognitive behavioural techniques*, Little, Brown Group, London.
- Orsillo, S. and Roemer, L. (2010). *The Mindful Way Through Anxiety: Break free from chronic worry and reclaim your life*, Guilford, New York.

Websites:

- New Zealand: Anxiety New Zealand Trust (www.anxiety. org.nz/about-us).
- United Kingdom: Anxiety UK (www.anxietyuk.org.uk).
- USA: Anxiety.org (www.anxiety.org) or the Anxiety and Depression Association of America (www.adaa.org).
- Australia: MindSpot (https://mindspot.org.au), Mindfulness (www.actmindfully.com.au/), cognitive behaviour therapy (www.cci.health.wa.gov.au).

Apps:

- 'Mind Mechanic' with relaxation tools for men or 'Smiling Mind' for mindfulness (www.smilingmind.com.au) or The Breathing App.

4. OVERCOMING DEPRESSION

Online depression self-test: The Black Dog Institute has a brief self-test to help you assess whether you have symptoms of depression and other related problems. It does not take the place of professional clinical advice (www.blackdoginstitute.org.au/ clinical-resources/depression/depression-self-test).

Reach out for assistance and learn more about depression:
There are a number of resources you can access:

Books:

- Bates, T. (2011). *Coming Through Depression*, Gill & MacMillan, Dublin.
- Edelman, S. (2013). *Change Your Thinking: Positive and practical ways to overcome stress, negative emotions and self-defeating behaviour using CBT*, HarperCollins Publishing, Sydney.
- Greenberger, D. and Padesky, C. (2016). *Mind Over Mood: Change how you feel by changing the way you think* (2nd edn), Guilford Press, New York.
- Hari, J. (2018). *Lost Connections: Uncovering the real causes of depression — and the unexpected solutions*, Bloomsbury Circus, London.
- Harris, R. and Aisbett, B. (2013). *The Happiness Trap Pocketbook*, Exisle Publishing, Wollombi, New South Wales.
- Manson, M. (2016). *The Subtle Art of Not Giving a F*ck: A counterintuitive approach to living a good life*, Macmillan Australia, Sydney.
- Segal, Z., Williams, M. and Teasdale, J. (2018). *Mindfulness-based Cognitive Therapy for Depression* (2nd edn), Guilford Press, New York.

Websites:

- New Zealand: Mental Health Foundation of New Zealand (www.mentalhealth.org.nz/get-help/a-z).
- South Africa: The South African Depression and Anxiety Group (www.sadag.org/).
- United Kingdom: Mental Health Foundation (www.mentalhealth.org.uk).
- USA: National Institute of Mental Health (www.nimh.nih.gov/health/topics/depression/index.shtml).
- Australia: Head to Health (www.headtohealth.gov.au), Beyond Blue (www.beyondblue.org.au) and BluePages depression information (www.bluepages.anu.edu.au).

- Mindfulness resources: ACT Mindfully (www.actmindfully. com.au/), Smiling Mind (www.smilingmind.com.au).
- Cognitive Behaviour Therapy: Centre for Clinical Interventions (www.cci.health.wa.gov.au/), and useful tools (www.getselfhelp.co.uk).
- Resources for new fathers: https://mensline.org.au/ being-a-dad/being-a-young-father/.
- Examples of online programs include Ecouch Cognitive Behaviour Therapy program (https://ecouch.anu. edu.au/new_users/mhl_portal/info), This Way Up (https://thiswayup.org.au/) and the Black Dog Institute (https://www.blackdoginstitute.org.au/getting-help/ self-help-tools-apps/mycompass).

Apps:
- 'Mind Mechanic' with relaxation tools for men, and the suicide prevention app called 'BeyondNow Suicide Safety Plan'.

5. MANAGING SUBSTANCE-RELATED ISSUES AND ADDICTIONS

Substance-related issues: There are a number of online resources you can access:
- World Health Organization (www.who.int/gho/ substance_abuse/en/).
- Australia: Australian Institute of Health and Welfare (www.aihw.gov.au/reports-data/behaviours-risk-factors/ illicit-use-of-drugs/reports).
- USA: Substance Abuse and Mental Health Services Administration (www.samhsa.gov/find-help/atod).
- Europe: European Monitoring Centre for Drugs and Drug Addiction (www.emcdda.europa.eu).
- New Zealand: New Zealand Drug Foundation (https:// www.drugfoundation.org.nz/info/).

Core beliefs in substance use: The Centre for Clinical Interventions (www.cci.health.wa.gov.au) has good resources on this.

Do you have an issue with substance use? The AUDIT questionnaire can be found at https://auditscreen.org/. It is an effective tool for screening for excessive alcohol use.

Motivational interviewing: See https://drugabuse. com/treatment-therapy/motivational-interviewing/ and www.psychologytoday.com/au/therapy-types/ motivational-interviewing.

Relapse prevention: Smart Recovery has useful information about relapse or 'backsliding' (www.smartrecovery.org/ smart-recovery-toolbox/how-to-deal-with-backsliding).

Addiction: There are a number of resources you can access:
Books:
- Brand, R. (2017). *Recovery: Freedom from our addictions*, Bluebird, London.
- Noffs, M. and Palmer, K. (2018). *Addicted? How addiction affects every one of us and what we can do about it*, HarperCollins, Australia.
- Williams, R. and Kraft, J. (2012). *The Mindfulness Workbook for Addiction: A guide to coping with the grief, stress and anger that trigger addictive behaviors*, New Harbinger, USA.

Websites:
- Australia: Health Direct (www.healthdirect.gov.au/ substance-abuse) and the Alcohol and Drug Foundation (https://adf.org.au/resources/drug-information-directory/).
- New Zealand: New Zealand Drug Foundation (www. drugfoundation.org.nz/info/).
- Canada: Canadian Centre on Substance Use and Addiction (www.ccsa.ca/).

- USA: Substance Abuse and Mental Health Services Administration (https://www.samhsa.gov/treatment/substance-use-disorders).

Gambling There are a number of online resources you can access:
- Australia: Lifeline (www.lifeline.org.au/get-help/topics/problem-gambling).
- USA: HelpGuide (www.helpguide.org/articles/addictions/gambling-addiction-and-problem-gambling.htm), SMART Recovery (www.smartrecovery.org/smart-recovery-toolbox/) and National Council on Problem Gambling (www.ncpgambling.org/programs-resources/).
- United Kingdom: Gambling Commission (www.gamblingcommission.gov.uk/for-the-public/Safer-gambling/Getting-help-to-control-your-gambling.aspx).
- New Zealand: Gambling Helpline New Zealand (www.gamblinghelpline.co.nz).

6. DEALING WITH UNCOMFORTABLE FEELINGS (SUCH AS ANGER AND GRIEF)

Guilt and Shame: Check out Brené Brown's TED talk 'The Power of Vulnerability' (www.youtube.com/watch?v=iCvmsMzlF7o) and her other YouTube videos, or her book *Daring Greatly: How the courage to be vulnerable transforms the way we live, love, parent, and lead,* (Avery, 2012) or Joseph Burgo's book *Shame: Free yourself, find joy and build true self-esteem,* (St Martin's Essentials, 2018).

Anger: There are a number of resources you can access:
Books:
- Masters, R. (2018). *To Be a Man: A guide to true masculine power*, Sounds True, Boulder.

Websites:
- Australia: Australian Psychological Society (www.psychology.org.au) and MensLine Australia (https://mensline.org.au/).

- USA: American Psychological Association (www.apa.org/topics/anger/control) and HelpGuide (www.helpguide.org/articles/relationships-communication/anger-management.htm#).
- United Kingdom: National Health Service (www.nhs.uk/conditions/stress-anxiety-depression/controlling-anger/).
- New Zealand: Mental Health Foundation (www.mentalhealth.org.nz/get-help/a-z/resource/42/anger).

Loss and grief: There are a number of resources you can access:

Book:

- McKissock, D. and McKissock, M. (2018). *Coping with Grief* (5th edn), ABC Books, Sydney.

Websites:

- Australia: Australian Centre for Grief and Bereavement (www.grief.org.au/resources) and GriefLink (www.grieflink.org.au).
- USA: US National Library of Medicine (https://medlineplus.gov/bereavement.html).
- United Kingdom: Mind for Better Mental Health (www.mind.org.uk/information-support/guides-to-support-and-services/bereavement/about-bereavement/).
- New Zealand: The Grief Centre (www.mentalhealth.org.nz/assets/A-Z/Downloads/Grief-after-loss-Grief-Centre-NZ.pdf).

Tolerating emotional distress: There are a number of resources you can access:

Books:

- McKay, M. and Wood, J. (2011). *The Dialectical Behaviour Therapy Diary: Monitoring your emotional regulation day by day*, New Harbinger Publications, California.
- Olivo, E. (2014). *Wise Mind Living: Master your emotions, transform your life*. Sounds True, Boulder.

Websites:

- Australia: Centre for Clinical Interventions modules (www.cci.health.wa.gov.au/Resources/Looking-After-Yourself/Tolerating-Distress).
- United Kingdom: Get Self Help (www.getselfhelp.co.uk).

Dialectical behaviour therapy: (www.dbtselfhelp.com/html/self-sooth.html and www.youtube.com/watch?v=sJrgPC11VS0).

7. THE IMPACT OF TRAUMA AND DISASTER ON MEN

Post-traumatic stress disorder: Phoenix Australia has guidelines and downloads for assessing and treating post-traumatic stress disorder: (www.phoenixaustralia.org/resources/ptsd-guidelines/) and the PCL-5 is a self-report measure that assesses the symptoms of post-traumatic stress disorder. It is available at (www.ptsd.va.gov/professional/assessment/adult-sr/ptsd-checklist.asp#obtain).

Complex trauma: You can learn more about complex trauma at: www.traumadissociation.com/complexptsd.html.

Recovery from trauma: There are a number of online resources you can access:

- Australia: Phoenix Australia Guidelines on Management of PTSD (http://phoenixaustralia.org/resources/ptsd-guidelines/), Department of Veterans' Affairs Open Arms portal (https://www.openarms.gov.au/) and app (https://www.openarms.gov.au/resources/mobile-apps).
- USA: Substance and Mental Health Services Administration (https://store.samhsa.gov/product/SAMHSA-s-Concept-of-Trauma-and-Guidance-for-a-Trauma-Informed-Approach/SMA14-4884.html) and Refugee Health (https://refugeehealthta.org/physical-mental-health/mental-health/adult-mental-health/traumatic-experiences-of-refugees/).
- United Kingdom: ASSIST Trauma Care (http://assisttraumacare.org.uk/our-service/) and Mind for Better Mental Health (www.mind.org.uk/)

- New Zealand: Skylight (www.skylight.org.nz/resources/ trauma/trauma-recovery).

8 WORKING ON RELATIONSHIP ISSUES

Ways to maintain a healthy partner relationship: Helpful books or websites include:

Books:
- Chapman, G. (2010). *The 5 Love Languages: The secret to love that lasts.* Northfield Publishing, Chicago.
- Gottman, J. M. and Silver, N. (2007). *The Seven Principles for Making Marriage Work: A practical guide from the country's foremost relationship expert.* Orion, London.
- Harris, R. (2009). *ACT with Love: Stop struggling, reconcile differences, and strengthen your relationship with acceptance and commitment therapy,* New Harbinger Publications, California.

Websites and blogs:
- Australia: Relationships Australia (www.relationships.org. au).
- USA: Psychology Today (www.psychologytoday.com/au/ blog/fulfillment-any-age/201203/5-principles-effective-couples-therapy).
- New Zealand: Relationships NZ (www.relationships.org.nz/).
- United Kingdom: Mental Health Foundation (https:// www.mentalhealth.org.uk/publications/relationships-21st-century-forgotten-foundation-mental-health-and-wellbeing).

Performance anxiety: You can find a very good blog at: https://nationalsocialanxietycenter.com/2017/01/12/ sex-men-social-anxiety-male-sexual-performance-anxiety/.

Domestic violence: Online resources on domestic violence online include:
- USA: National Coalition Against Domestic Violence (www. ncadv.org).

- Australia: Reach Out (www.reachout.com/tough-times/bullying-abuse-and-violence) and White Ribbon Australia (www.whiteribbon.org.au/).
- South Africa: The South African Police Service has domestic violence information (www.saps.gov.za/resource_centre/women_children/domestic_violence.php).
- United Kingdom: United Kingdom Government (www.gov.uk/guidance/domestic-abuse-how-to-get-help).
- New Zealand: Relationships NZ (www.relationships.org.nz/blog/types-of-abuse).

Separation and divorce: Online resources on separation and divorce:
- Australia: MensLine Australia (https://mensline.org.au/) and Relationships Australia (www.relationships.org.au).
- New Zealand: Relationships NZ (www.relationships.org.nz/blog/types-of-abuse).
- USA: American Psychological Association (www.apa.org/topics/divorce/).

9. COMMON DISORDERS THAT AFFECT MEN'S MENTAL HEALTH

Autism: For further information on autism, refer to your national autism services. For example, the National Autistic Society in the United Kingdom (www.autism.org.uk/), Autism Awareness Australia (www.autismawareness.com.au/) and the Autism Society in the USA (www.autism-society.org/). These societies generally put out a range of information sheets and handbooks.

Attention disorders: An excellent resource is a book by Greg Crosby and Tonya Lippert called *Transforming ADHD: Simple, effective attention and action regulation skills to help you focus and succeed* (New Harbinger Publications, 2006). It provides great tips and tools and lists various apps to help block internet distractions and to stay on task. Other resources on attention disorders can be found online at:

- Australia: ADHD Australia (www.adhdaustralia.org.au/about-adhd/what-is-attention-deficit-hyperactivity-disorder-adhd/).
- New Zealand: Mental Health Foundation of New Zealand (www.mentalhealth.org.nz).
- USA: CHADD (https://chadd.org/).
- United Kingdom: National Health Service (www.nhs.uk/conditions/attention-deficit-hyperactivity-disorder-adhd/).

Eating disorders: Online resources on eating disorders can be found at:
- Australia: Mental Health First Aid (www.mhfa.com.au) and The Butterfly Foundation (https://thebutterflyfoundation.org.au/).
- USA: refer to the American Psychiatric Association (www.psychiatry.org/) and American Psychological Association (www.apa.org/) websites.
- United Kingdom: National Centre for Eating Disorders (www.eating-disorders.org.uk).
- New Zealand: Mental Health Foundation of New Zealand (www.mentalhealth.org.nz).

Body dysmorphia: Online resources on body dysmorphia include:
- USA: The Mayo Clinic (www.mayoclinic.org).
- Australia: Centre for Clinical Interventions (www.cci.health.wa.gov.au/Resources/Looking-After-Yourself/Body-Dysmorphia).

Psychosis: Online resources on psychosis include:
- Australia: Mental Health First Aid Australia (https://mhfa.com.au/sites/default/files/MHFA_psychosis_guidelines_A4_2012.pdf) and SANE Australia (www.sane.org).
- USA: HelpGuide (www.helpguide.org/articles/mental-disorders/schizophrenia-treatment-and-self-help.htm).
- New Zealand: Mental Health Foundation of New Zealand (www.mentalhealth.org.nz).

- United Kingdom: National Health Service (www.nhs.uk/conditions/psychosis/).

Dementia: Online resources on dementia include:
- World Health Organization (www.who.int) has guidelines on reducing the risks of dementia.
- Australia: Dementia Australia (www.dementia.org.au) lists the National Dementia Helpline and features help sheets in various languages.
- United Kingdom: Alzheimer's Society (www.alzheimers.org.uk/about-dementia/five-things-you-should-know-about-dementia).
- USA: Alzheimer's Association (www.alz.org/alzheimer_s_dementia).
- New Zealand: Dementia NZ (https://dementia.nz/)

10. PREVENTING SUICIDE AND DEALING WITH NON-SUICIDAL SELF-HARM

Suicide prevention: Online resources on suicide prevention include:
- Australia: Mental Health First Aid Australia (https://mhfa.com.au/), Living Is For Everyone (LIFE) (www.livingisforeveryone.com.au/), Life in Mind Aboriginal and Torres Strait Island Communities (www.lifeinmindaustralia.com.au/about-suicide/aboriginal-and-torres-strait-islander-communities).
- New Zealand: Mental Health Foundation of New Zealand (http://www.mentalhealth.org.nz/get-help/a-z).
- USA: American Foundation for Suicide Prevention (www.afsp.org).
- United Kingdom: National Health Service has information on suicide prevention (www.nhs.uk/conditions/suicide/pages/introduction.aspx), and self-harm (www.nhs.uk/conditions/self-injury/pages/introduction.aspx). Mental Health Foundation (www.mentalhealth.org.uk/a-to-z/s/suicide).

- South Africa: South African Depression and Anxiety Group (www.sadag.org).

Help for the family or significant others: There is an excellent book called *After Suicide: Help for the bereaved* by Dr Sheila Clark (ReadHowYouWant, 2013) that is very useful. The following websites may also assist:
- Australia: Grieflink (https://grieflink.org.au/grief-and-suicide/) and Support after Suicide (www.supportaftersuicide.org.au/).

Non-suicidal self-harm: Online resources on non-suicidal self-harm include:
- Australia: Mental Health First Aid Australia (mhfa.com.au/mental-health-first-aid-guidelines), Reach Out (https://au.reachout.com/tough-times/self-harm) and Headspace (headspace.org.au/).
- New Zealand: Mental Health Foundation of New Zealand (www.mentalhealth.org.nz/get-help/a-z)
- USA: Mental Health America (www.mhanational.org/conditions/self-injury-cutting-self-harm-or-self-mutilation).
- United Kingdom: National Health Service has information on self-harm (www.nhs.uk/conditions/self-injury/pages/introduction.aspx).

11. PREVENTING MENTAL HEALTH ISSUES AND FOSTERING SELF-BELIEF

Resilience: Resources on resilience include:
Books:
- Fredrickson, B. (2009). *Positivity: Groundbreaking research to release your inner optimist and thrive,* Oneworld Publications, London.
- Hanson, R. (2018). *Resilient: Find your inner strength.* Rider, London.
- Lyubomirsky, S. (2007). *The How of Happiness: A new approach to getting the life you want,* Sphere, London.
- Poulson, I. (2008). *Rise.* Macmillan Australia, Sydney.

- Schiraldi, G. (2017). *The Resilience Workbook: Essential skills to recover from stress, trauma, and adversity.* New Harbinger Publications, California.
- Seligman, M. (2011). *Flourish.* Random House Australia, Sydney (see also Seligman's website (www. authentichappiness.sas.upenn.edu).

REFERENCES

1. ABOUT MEN'S MENTAL HEALTH

1. WHO (2014). 'Mental health: a state of wellbeing,' retrieved October 2018 from World Health Organization: www.who.int.
2. Simon-Davies, J. (2019). International Men's Health Week, retrieved 2019 from Australian Bureau of Statistics: www.aph.gov.au/About_Parliament/Parliamentary_Departments/Parliamentary_Library/FlagPost/2019/June/Mens_health.
3. Rice, S. M., Fallon, B. J., Aucote, H. M. and Möller-Leimkühler, A. M. (2013). 'Development and preliminary validation of the male depression risk scale: Furthering the assessment of depression in men,' *Journal of Affective Disorders*, 151(3), pp. 950–58.
4. Grant, J. and Potenza, M. (2007). *Textbook of Men's Mental Health*, American Psychiatric Publishing, Inc., Washington, p. 369.
5. Dent, M. (2018). *Mothering Our Boys: A guide for mums of sons*, Pennington Publications, Gerringong.
6. Brown, B. (2012). *Men, Women & Worthiness*, Sounds True, Louisville.
7. Robinson, M. (2019). 'What is Toxic Masculinity?', retrieved from *The Book of Man*: https://thebookofman.com/mind/masculinity/what-is-toxic-masculinity/
8. Grayburn, T. (2017). *Boys Don't Cry: A story of love, depression and men*, Hodder and Stoughton, London.
9. Brown, B. (2012). *Daring Greatly: How the courage to be vulnerable transforms the way we live, love, parent, and lead*, Penguin Books, London.
10. Masters, R. (2018). *To Be a Man: A guide to true masculine power*, Sounds True, Boulder.
11. Ian Thorpe quote from '30 years, 30 Great Australians,' (2018). *The Weekend Australian*, pp. 15–16. Interviews by Greg Bearup, Trent Dalton, Richard Guilliatt, Kate Legge, Megan Lehmann, Nick Tabakoff, Sarah-Jane Tasker and Glynis Traill-Nash.

2. TWELVE KEY TOOLS TO IMPROVE YOUR MENTAL HEALTH

1. Hanson, R. (2013). *Hardwiring Happiness: The new brain science of contentment, calm, and confidence*, Rider Books, London.
2. Santini, Z., Koyanagi, A., Tyrovolas, S., Mason, C. and Haro, J. (2015). 'The association between social relationships and depression: A systematic review,' *Journal of Affective Disorders*, 175, pp. 53–65.

3. TACKLING STRESS AND ANXIETY

1. O'Keeffe, D. (2017). 'Financial Stress: We're worrying ourselves sick over money,' retrieved August 2018 from ABC News: www.abc.net.au/news/health/2017-02-10/financial-stress-worrying-ourselves-sick-over-money/8258784.
2. Hari, J. (2018). *Lost Connections: Uncovering the real causes of depression — the unexpected solutions*, Bloomsbury Circus, London.
3. McCanny, C. (n.d.). 'Anxiety Within Sport,' retrieved December 2018 from BelievePerform: https://believeperform.com/performance/anxiety-within-sport/.
4. Segal, Z. (2019). 'A 7-Minute Mindfulness Practice to Shift out of "Doing" Mode," retrieved from mindful: www.mindful.org/a-7-minute-practice-to-shift-out-of-doing-mode/.
5. Harris, R. (2019). *ACT Made Simple: An easy-to-read primer on acceptance and commitment therapy*, 2nd edn, New Harbinger Publications Inc., Oakland.

4. OVERCOMING DEPRESSION

1. 'Sporting Stars' Battle with Clinical Depression.' (2017). Retrieved from Australian Genetics of Depression Study: www.geneticsofdepression.org.au/sporting-stars-battle-with-clinical-depression/.
2. Bertin, M. (2016). 'Mental Meteorology: How noticing your thoughts leads to healthier habits of mind,' retrieved from mindful: www.mindful.org/mental-meteorology-noticing-thoughts-leads-healthier-habits-mind/.
3. Goldstein, E. (2016). '3 Mindful Ways to Transform Negative Thoughts,' retrieved from mindful: www.mindful.org/3-simple-ways-transform-negative-thoughts/.
4. Penman, D. (2011). 'Curing Depression with Mindfulness Meditation: A longer lasting solution to the spiral of sadness,' retrieved from Psychology Today: www.psychologytoday.com/us/blog/mindfulness-in-frantic-world/201110/curing-depression-mindfulness-meditation.

5. Harris, R. (2019). *ACT Made Simple: An easy-to-read primer on acceptance and commitment therapy*, 2nd edn, New Harbinger Publications Inc., Oakland.

6. Centre for Clinical Interventions (www.cci.health.wa.gov.au/Resources/ Looking-After-Yourself/Perfectionism).

7. O'Reilly-Davi-Digui, K. (2018). 'Simple Living Tips for the Stressed Out or Recovering Perfectionist,' retrieved July 2019 from A Life in Progress: www.alifeinprogress.ca/simple-living-tips/.

8. Manson, M. (2016). *The Subtle Art of Not Giving a F*ck: A counterintuitive approach to living a good life*, Pan Macmillan Australia, Sydney.

5. MANAGING SUBSTANCE-RELATED ISSUES AND ADDICTIONS

1. 'Illicit Use of Drugs.' (2016). Retrieved from Australian Institute of Health and Welfare: www.aihw.gov.au/reports-data/behaviours-risk-factors/illicit-use-of-drugs/reports.

2. 'United Kingdom Country Drug Report 2019,' retrieved January 2020 from www.emcdda.europa.eu.

3. Kelly, W. (2018). 'The Drug Problem in the U.S. Is Not What We Think It Is,' retrieved June 2019 from Psychology Today: www.psychologytoday. com/us/blog/crime-and-punishment/201809/the-drug-problem-in-the-us-is-not-what-we-think-it-is.

4. Drug Use in New Zealand. (n.d.). Retrieved 8 March 2020 from www. drugfoundation.org.nz/policy-and-advocacy/drugs-in-nz-an-overview/.

5. headspace for health professionals. (n.d.). Retrieved March 2017 from headspace: https://headspace.org.au/health-professionals/ understanding-substance-abuse-for-health-professionals/.

6. Ellen, S. and Deveny, C. (2018). *Mental: Everything you never knew you needed to know about mental health*, Black Inc., Carlton.

7. 'Disorders Due to Substance Use.' (2019). Retrieved from ICD-11 for Mortality and Morbidity Statistics: https://icd.who.int/browse11/l-m/ en#/http%3a%2f%2fid.who.int%2ficd%2fentity%2f590211325.

8. 'Illicit Use of Drugs.' (2016). Retrieved from Australian Institute of Health and Welfare: www.aihw.gov.au/reports-data/behaviours-risk-factors/illicit-use-of-drugs/reports.

9. Lewis, T. (2014). 'Substance Abuse and Addiction Treatment: Practical application of counseling theory,' retrieved from www.pearson.com/us/ higher-education/program/Lewis-Substance-Abuse-and-Addiction-Treatment-Practical-Application-of-Counseling-Theory-My-Lab-

Counseling-without-Pearson-e-Text-Access-Card-Package/PGM38164.
html.

10. Lewis, T. (2014). 'Substance Abuse and Addiction Treatment: Practical
    application of counseling theory,' retrieved from www.pearson.com/us/
    higher-education/program/Lewis-Substance-Abuse-and-Addiction-
    Treatment-Practical-Application-of-Counseling-Theory-My-Lab-
    Counseling-without-Pearson-e-Text-Access-Card-Package/PGM38164.
    html.

11. Grant, J. and Potenza, M. (2007). *Textbook of Men's Mental Health*,
    American Psychiatric Publishing, Inc., Washington, p. 209.

12. Ellen, S. and Deveny, C. (2018). *Mental: Everything you never knew you
    needed to know about mental health*, Black Inc., Carlton, p. 154.

13. Ellen, S. and Deveny, C. (2018). *Mental: Everything you never knew you
    needed to know about mental health*, Black Inc., Carlton, p. 155.

14. Legg, T. (2019). 'Everything You Need to Know About Pornography
    "Addiction",' retrieved June 2019 from healthline: www.healthline.com/
    health/pornography-addiction.

15. Legg, T. (2019). 'Everything You Need to Know About Pornography
    "Addiction",' retrieved June 2019 from healthline: www.healthline.com/
    health/pornography-addiction.

16. Rauch, J. (2017). 'Porn Addiction Therapy: What you need to know,'
    retrieved June 2019 from TalkSpace: www.talkspace.com/blog/porn-
    addiction-therapy-need-know/.

17. Cunningham, M. (2019). 'Trapped in the Net: Are we all addicted to our
    smartphones?' retrieved from *Sunday Age*: www.theage.com.au/national/
    victoria/trapped-in-the-net-are-we-all-addicted-to-our-smartphones-
    20190531-p51t44.html.

18. Smith, M., Robinson, L. and Segal, J. (2019). 'Smartphone Addiction,'
    retrieved July 2019 from HelpGuide: www.helpguide.org/articles/
    addictions/smartphone-addiction.htm.

19. Grohol, J. (2018). 'FOMO Addiction: The fear of missing out,' retrieved
    May 2019 from PsychCentral: https://psychcentral.com/blog/fomo-
    addiction-the-fear-of-missing-out/.

6. DEALING WITH UNCOMFORTABLE FEELINGS (SUCH AS ANGER AND GRIEF)

1. Baker, R. 'What Our Boys Need to Hear,' *The Advertiser*, 4 August 2019.
2. Brown, B. (2012). *Daring Greatly: How the courage to be vulnerable
   transforms the way we live, love, parent, and lead*, Penguin Books,
   London.

3. Burgo, J. (2018). *Shame: Free yourself, find joy, and build true self-esteem*, St Martin's Essentials, New York.

4. Masters, R. (2018). *To Be a Man: A guide to true masculine power*. Sounds True, Boulder.

5. Madigan, N. (2019). 'Mental Health Experts Vital in the Fight Against Domestic Violence,' from HealthTimes: https://healthtimes.com.au/hub/mental-health/37/practice/nm/mental-health-experts-vital-in-the-fight-against-domestic-violence/4232/.

6. Scanlan, F., Parker, A. and Montague, A. (2016). 'Understanding and Assessing Anger-related Difficulties in Young People,' from Orygen: www.orygen.org.au/Training/Resources/Clinical-complexity/Evidence-summary/Understanding-and-assessing-anger/Orygen-Understanding-and-Assessing-Anger-Related-I?ext=.

7. Conrad, D. and White, A. (2010). *Promoting Men's Mental Health*, Taylor & Francis Ltd, London.

8. 'Anger Management: Williams' 12 strategies for controlling aggression,' retrieved July 2019 from MindTools: www.mindtools.com/pages/article/newTCS_97.htm.

9. Bull, M. (2009). 'Loss' in Barkway, P. (ed.), *Psychology for Health Professionals*, Elsevier, Sydney, p. 207.

10. McKay, M. and Wood, J. (2011). *The Dialectical Behaviour Therapy Diary: Monitoring your emotional regulation day by day*, New Harbinger Publications, Oakland.

11. Vivyan, C. (2009). 'Unhelpful Thinking Habits,' retrieved from Get Self Help UK: www.getselfhelp.co.uk/docs/UnhelpfulThinkingHabitsWithAlt ernatives.pdf.

12. McKay, M. and Wood, J. (2011). *The Dialectical Behaviour Therapy Diary: Monitoring your emotional regulation day by day*, New Harbinger Publications, Oakland.

7. THE IMPACT OF TRAUMA AND DISASTER ON MEN

1. SAMHSA-HRSA Center for Integrated Health Solutions. (n.d.). Retrieved from Trauma: www.integration.samhsa.gov/clinical-practice/trauma.

2. Grant, J. and Potenza, M. (2007). *Textbook of Men's Mental Health*, American Psychiatric Publishing, Inc., Washington, p. 235.

3. Hughes, K., Bellis, M., Hardcastle K., et al. (2017). 'The effect of multiple adverse childhood experiences on health: A systemic review and meta-analysis,' *The Lancet*, 2(8), pp. 356–66.

4. 'Understanding the Effects of Maltreatment on Brain Development.'

(2015). Retrieved July 2019 from Child Welfare Information Gateway: www.childwelfare.gov/pubs/issue-briefs/brain-development.

5. 'PTSD Guidelines.' (n.d.). Retrieved July 2019 from Phoenix Australia: www.phoenixaustralia.org/resources/ptsd-guidelines/.

6. 'National Comorbidity Survey (NCS).' Harvard Medical School (2005). Retrieved 21 August 2017 from www.hcp.med.harvard.edu/ncs/index. php: Data Table 1: Lifetime prevalence of DSM-IV/WMH-CIDI disorders by sex and cohort: www.hcp.med.harvard.edu/ncs/ftpdir/NCS-R_Lifetime_Prevalence_Estimates.pdf.

7. Taylor, S. (2017). *Clinicians Guide to PTSD: A cognitive-behavioural approach* 2nd edn, The Guilford Press, New York.

8. Swaby, S. (2016). 'How Men Face Their Trauma' retrieved from The Good Men Project: https://goodmenproject.com/featured-content/men-face-trauma-snsw/.

9. Wingard, B., Johnson, C. and Drahm-Butler, T. (2015). *Aboriginal Narrative Practice: Honouring storylines of pride, strength and creativity*, Dulwich Centre Publications, Adelaide.

8. WORKING ON RELATIONSHIP ISSUES

1. Grant, J. and Potenza, M. (2007). *Textbook of Men's Mental Health*, American Psychiatric Publishing, Inc., Washington, p. 284.

2. Chapman, G. (1992). *The 5 Love Languages*, Northfield Publishing, Chicago.

3. Harris, R. (2009). *ACT with Love: Stop struggling, reconcile differences, and strengthen your relationship with acceptance and commitment therapy*, New Harbinger Publications, Oakland, p. 147.

4. Harris, V. (n.d.). '9 Important Communication Skills for Every Relationship,' retrieved from EDIS: https://edis.ifas.ufl.edu/fy1277.

5. Harris, R. (2009). *ACT with Love: Stop struggling, reconcile differences, and strengthen your relationship with acceptance and commitment therapy*, New Harbinger Publications, Oakland, p. 181.

6. Harris, R. (2009). *ACT with Love: Stop struggling, reconcile differences, and strengthen your relationship with acceptance and commitment therapy*, New Harbinger Publications, Oakland, p. 36.

7. Grant, J. and Potenza, M. (2007). *Textbook of Men's Mental Health*, American Psychiatric Publishing, Washington, p. 286.

8. Harris, R. (2009). *ACT with Love: Stop struggling, reconcile differences, and strengthen your relationship with acceptance and commitment therapy*, New Harbinger Publications, Oakland, p. 131.

9. Harris, R. (2009). *ACT with Love: Stop struggling, reconcile differences,*

and strengthen your relationship with acceptance and commitment therapy, New Harbinger Publications, Oakland, p. 141.

10. Gottman, J. and Silver, N. (2007). *The Seven Principles for Making Marriage Work*, Orion Books, London, p. 260.

11. Whitbourne, S. (2017). 'The Secret Reason Why Sex Is So Crucial in Relationships,' retrieved August 2019 from Psychology Today: www.psychologytoday.com/au/blog/fulfillment-any-age/201707/the-secret-reason-why-sex-is-so-crucial-in-relationships.

12. Grant, J. and Potenza, M. (2007). *Textbook of Men's Mental Health*, American Psychiatric Publishing, Inc., Washington, p. 290.

13. Stritof, S. (2020). '5 Common Types of Affairs', retrieved March 2020 from verywellmind: www.verywellmind.com/marriage-affair-2303083.

14. 'What is domestic violence?' (n.d.). Retrieved August 2019 from White Ribbon Australia: www.whiteribbon.org.au/understand-domestic-violence/what-is-domestic-violence/.

15. Grant, J. and Potenza, M. (2007). *Textbook of Men's Mental Health*, American Psychiatric Publishing, Inc., Washington, p. 295.

16. White, C. (2010). 'The Forms of Attachment,' retrieved June 2019 from Essential Parenting: www.essentialparenting.com/2010/05/22/the-forms-of-attachment.

17. Hussey, R. (2016). '14 Things You Need to Know about Adult Attachment Theory,' retrieved June 2019 from Art of wellbeing: www.artofwellbeing.com/2016/09/02/attachmenttheory/.

9. COMMON DISORDERS THAT AFFECT MEN'S MENTAL HEALTH

1. Casanova, E. and Casanova, M. (2019). *Defining Autism: A guide to brain, biology and behavior*, Jessica Kingsley Publishers, London.

2. Foley, K. and Troller, J. (2015). 'Management of mental ill health in people with autism spectrum disorder,' *Australian Family Physician*, 44(11), pp. 784–90.

3. Crosby, B. and Lippert, T. (2006). *Transforming ADHD: Simple, effective attention and action regulation skills to help you focus and succeed*, New Harbinger Publications, Oakland, pp. 122–25.

4. 'Our Sons Need More Support with Body Image Issues.' (2017). Retrieved from www.understandingboys.com.au/our-sons-need-more-support-with-body-image-issues/.

10. PREVENTING SUICIDE AND DEALING WITH NON-SUICIDAL SELF-HARM

1. 'Suicide facts and stats.' (2019). Retrieved from Life in Mind: www.lifeinmindaustralia.com.au/about-suicide/suicide-data/suicide-facts-and-stats.

2. 'Mental Health First Aid Guidelines.' (2014). Retrieved from Mental Health First Aid Australia: https://mhfa.com.au/mental-health-first-aid-guidelines.

3. 'Mental Health First Aid Guidelines.' (2014). Retrieved from Mental Health First Aid Australia: https://mhfa.com.au/mental-health-first-aid-guidelines.

4. Ellen, S. and Deveny, C. (2018). *Mental: Everything you never knew you needed to know about mental health*, Black Inc., Carlton, p. 157.

5. Commonwealth of Australia. (2007). *Foundations for Effective Practice: Square suicide questions answers resources* at www.square.org.au/wp-content/uploads/sites/10/2013/05/Foundations-of-Effective-Practice_May2013.pdf.

6. Ellen, S. and Deveny, C. (2018). *Mental: Everything you never knew you needed to know about mental health*, Black Inc., Carlton, p. 158.

7. Balaratnasingam, S. (2011). 'Mental Health Risk Assessment: A guide for GPs,' *Australian Family Physician*, 40(6), pp. 366–69.

8. Westers, N., Muehlenkamp, N. and Lau, M. (2016). 'SOARS Model of Risk Assessment in Non-suicidal Self-Injury,' *Contemporary Paediatrics*, 33(7), pp. 25–31.

9. Swift, B. (2017). 'Nonsuicidal Self-Injury: Proper identification and treatment,' retrieved from Psychiatry Advisor: www.psychiatryadvisor.com/home/topics/suicide-and-self-harm/nonsuicidal-self-injury-proper-identification-and-treatment/.

10. 'Mental Health First Aid Guidelines.' (2014). Retrieved from Mental Health First Aid Australia: https://mhfa.com.au/mental-health-first-aid-guidelines.

11. 'Mental Health First Aid Guidelines.' (2014). Retrieved from Mental Health First Aid Australia: https://mhfa.com.au/mental-health-first-aid-guidelines.

12. 'Self-Help for Self-Harm,' retrieved 8 March 2020 from ReachOut: https://au.reachout.com/articles/self-help-for-self-harm.

11. PREVENTING MENTAL HEALTH ISSUES AND FOSTERING SELF-BELIEF

1. Rauch, J. (2019). *The Happiness Curve: Why life gets better after midlife*, Green Tree, London.
2. 'Men and Emotions.' (n.d.). Retrieved July 2019 from MensLine Australia: https://mensline.org.au/mens-mental-health/men-and-emotions/.
3. 'Can Relationships Boost Longevity and Well-being?' (2017). Retrieved from Harvard Health Letter: www.health.harvard.edu/mental-health/can-relationships-boost-longevity-and-well-being.
4. Santini, Z., Koyanagi, A., Tyrovolas, S., Mason, C. and Haro, J. (2015). 'The association between social relationships and depression: A systematic review,' *Journal of Affective Disorders*, 175, pp. 53–65.
5. Biddulph, S. (2019). *The New Manhood: Love, freedom, spirit and the new masculinity*, Simon & Schuster Australia, Sydney, p. 204.
6. Buettner, D. (2008). *The Blue Zones: Lessons for living longer from the people who've lived the longest*, National Geographic, Washington.

FINAL WORDS

1. Mitchell, J. (2017). 'What's Your Wellbeing Plan?' retrieved 1 May 2019 from The Mind Room: https://themindroom.com.au/2017/03/21/whats-your-wellbeing-plan/.

ACKNOWLEDGEMENTS

There are a number of wonderful people to acknowledge and thank. We are very grateful to Dr Chris Holmwood and Dr Hsuen Lee, who offered their expertise to us so generously during the writing of this book.

Thanks to Nick who assisted with many useful ideas on men's mental health, and to another Nick who read an early draft and provided useful feedback.

A special 'thank you' to David who tirelessly read many drafts and provided a great deal of assistance and support along the way, and to Aileen who offered kind support. Special mention to Matilda who helped with referencing, which can be a tedious task!

Cate especially wishes to thank all of her clients over the years who have shared their stories and allowed her to travel alongside them in their recovery journeys.

And thank you to our publisher, who saw the importance of publishing a book about men's mental health and enabled us to share our knowledge with the community.

INDEX